⌂ HOMEWORK 2: OUTSIDE

⌂ HOMEWORK 2: OUTSIDE

Structures Publishing Company
Farmington, Michigan 48024

Editor Shirley Horowitz

Graphics Editor Carey Jean Ferchland

Current Printing (last digit)
10 9 8 7 6 5 4 3 2 1

Original Copyright © German Edition

Orbis Verlag/Verlagsgruppe Bertelsmann
2 Hamburg
Konrad Adenauerallee 9
WEST GERMANY

List of Projects

Foreword

The **HOMEWORK** series is a refreshing new approach to do-it-yourself projects. I call it **HOMEWORK** because the work is done at home with home workshop tools, and because the projects are all connected with the home in some way.

The first two volumes, **HOMEWORK 1: INSIDE** and **HOMEWORK 2: OUTSIDE**, are a distillation of the series called "Selbermachen" created by a German publisher, subtitled, "The Practical Handbook for Practical People." The selections for these two books represent the most attractive projects for English-language homeworkers, chosen from the five much larger "Selbermachen" volumes.

Future **HOMEWORK** books will be from the Selbermachen series and other foreign sources, as well as extracts from U.S. magazines not previously published in book form. We think we have found, and will find, more exciting and ingenious projects that will give the homeworker hours of rewarding work as well as finished projects the family can enjoy for years to come.

Since discovering the "Selbermachen" books at the Frankfurt International Book Fair, I have been humbled by the task that I undertook. The first step was to carefully select projects which would interest English-language homeworkers. Next, the text and the dimensions had to be translated from German.

Then, it fell to me as the author of "The American Metric Construction Handbook" to translate the translation. This means the translation of European sizes had to be converted to usages available and accepted in the U.S. and Canada.

For example, the text may call for a wood member that translates from the metric as $1^{15}/_{16}$" x $2^{7}/_{8}$"; there is no comparable U.S. size. But we do have a 2" x 3" ($1\frac{1}{2}$ x $2\frac{1}{2}$), so that a judgment must be made as to whether the 2" x 3" will do the job and whether abutting materials can accommodate a size change.

Most of this work has fallen to me and I beg your indulgence if you find an occasional error. Before you begin to assemble a project, it would be well to check to see that everything fits together, particularly if you choose to alter any dimension. If you find an error, or a better way to do it, please let me know, so we may modify future printings.

Why don't we show metric dimensions as well as inches? There are two reasons: some metric material sizes have not been determined in the U.S., and metric materials may not be available at your local source for some years.

We hope that you have many hours of recreation building these projects, and that you and yours will enjoy their beauty and utility in years to come.

R. J. Lytle
Publisher

MATERIALS

8 pieces	1 x 3 treated pine 72''
40 plywood strips	¼'' x 4'' x 22'', cut from sheets
8 pieces	1 x 3 treated pine 35½''
20 plywood strips	¼'' x 4'' x 61'', cut from sheets

3 pair hinges, galvanized
Wood preservative, waterproof glue.

A Portable Wind Screen

Enjoy the sunshine without the wind

The plywood can be purchased in sheets and cut to the 4 in. strips. Use ¼ in. exterior grade AA or AB Douglas Fir Plywood. Prior to weaving, we suggest that you apply a wood preservative to both the faces and the edges in order to insure long life.

You will need 16 blocks 1¾ in. x 1¾ in. as spacers for the weaving.

Lay out the vertical strips on a tabletop or other flat surface the size of the screen, and attach to one end with a piece of 2 x 4 and clamps. The first horizontal strip must be spaced 2½ in. from the edge at the end; ¾ in. of this will disappear in the grooves of the frame. This will leave the same screen line spacing as in the remaining panel.

The strips are clamped at their ends on the ¾ in. length. Then a row of spacer blocks is inserted between the strips and the first horizontal is woven in. Push flush against the blocks; adjust laterally; then install another row of blocks and the next horizontal strip, etc. When four rows have been completed, the blocks for the fifth row are taken out of the first row, etc.

The finished screen is

Only a few inexpensive materials are needed to build this windscreen of plywood. It protects against cool breezes and unwelcome spectators.

1. The spacing between the vertical strips of plywood is fixed with 1¾" blocks.

2. The first horizontal strip is inserted; then place another row of blocks, abut next strip flush, etc.

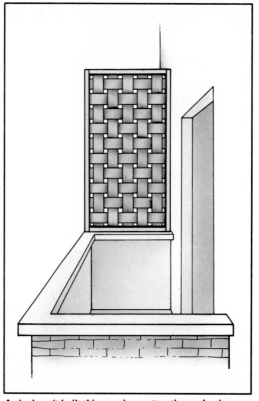

This is what an individual panel of the screen looks like. The corners are simple lap joints, that is the vertical and horizontal rails extend across the entire width and length of the frame.

A single unit built this way is an attractive and unique windscreen on the balcony. A smaller screen can be woven for indoor use.

3. The grooves are cut into the rail with a circular saw; depth is ¾". Two cuts are required for the ¼" plus width.

4. The recesses at the corners can also be "routed" with the circular saw by making several cuts. The depth is ½ the thickness of the board.

5. At the bottom of the vertical board remove the wood between the saw cuts with a chisel. A tight-fitting joint requires accuracy.

◄ **6.** The screen is clamped at one end with a piece of lumber; the frame rails can then be pushed onto the free ends of the strips.

7. The panels are connected to each other with a pair of hinges each. They should open alternately to the one side and the other.

quite stable by itself without glue, yet individual strips can be adjusted as needed. Use a piece of wood for this purpose, gently tapping with a hammer.

After all four panels have been woven, the grooves are routed into the rails of the frame, ¾ in. deep and a little over ¼ in. wide. One saw setting on your radial or table saw will do the job, running the piece through twice.

The recesses on the ends can be done similarly by making a series of cuts and then chiseling out the wood between.

The woven panels must be reclamped before the frame is attached. Carefully slide the frame rails in place in the sequence "side-bottom-side-top." Apply waterproof glue at the corners. Dowels or galvanized screws will provide additional stability.

If long clamps are not available, use rope and toggle.

Brick and block projects

Many attractive small or large scale projects can be made of brick, without mortar. Here is a flower tower of perforated brick set into the ground with a dowel or rod.

Perforated bricks can be used as kitchen organizers. The kitchen tools are close at hand, and decorative.

Brick, cement or cinder block, clay tile and other building units are made in a multitude of sizes and shapes. Shown here are European brick and block; U.S. sizes and hole arrangements are somewhat different but the basic idea will still work.

With standard sizes, various shapes can be combined. There are many possibilities for using plain brick. The examples on these pages are intended as suggestions that can spark your own creations.

Perforated bricks are particularly well suited for the flower tower or as storage elements. These bricks can be reinforced with wood or metal dowels. Simply drive the dowel, which should fit tightly, through the holes in the brick—down the entire length of the stack. You may choose to gain additional support by using grout, but then the components can no longer be disassembled or rearranged.

Hollow blocks of cement, cinder or other materials can easily be adapted to various uses. Large blocks are especially suitable as legs for tables and benches. Here, too, the holes should be reinforced with dowels. With some U.S. blocks you may wish to rip a 2 x 4 to size for this purpose.

Here is a tip for flower lovers: put a perforated brick into a glass container. Perfect for flower arranging!

12

With a few blocks and a grill, a barbecue grill can be improvised quickly. The charcoal rests on a patio block.
▼

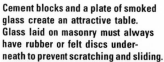
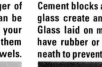

Try a unique wardrobe-hanger of perforated brick. Coat hooks can be purchased ready made at your do-it-yourself shop. Or make them out of dowels.

Cement blocks and a plate of smoked glass create an attractive table. Glass laid on masonry must always have rubber or felt discs underneath to prevent scratching and sliding.

A thin "Norman" brick makes a practical desk stand for pencils and pens. Felt underneath will keep it from scratching the desk.

A cozy, intimate light shines from this shelf lamp assembled of clay brick. It is easily rearranged.

This table top is made of glazed terra cotta tile. Cement blocks serve as legs, particleboard as support.

The tile are attached to the particleboard with grout. For edges, use corner molding or lattice, placed flush with the tile.

For the shelf unit shown —or any similar combination —it is important to choose undamaged block. The shelf unit is very stable and does not need to be attached to the wall due to reinforcement with dowels and the weight of the block.

Cement or cinder block can be protected from dust and dirt with commercially available sealers.

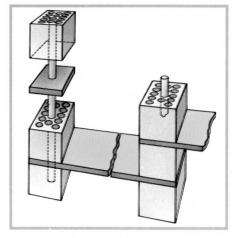

This shelf unit of boards and block is quickly assembled. If you use light colored block, or paint it white, the black stained shelves offer an effective contrast.

Vertical dowels give the unit additional stability. They are inserted through the holes into the block and the boards.

Portable Folding Table

Here is a folding table you can proudly admit you built yourself. As you can see in the picture, the table when folded down is only 4½ in. x 5 in. x 36 in. It takes only a minute to set up; then it opens to 36 in. x 28 in. and seats four easily.

Using a ⅛" drill, drill halfway through each tabletop board from each edge. Holes will meet to go all the way through the board.

Using a ⅝" router bit, cut slots ½" deep in mounting boards so they can receive table legs.

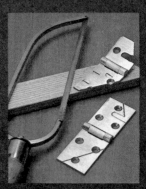

A hacksaw will transform brass hinges for use as support braces.

Five minutes spent now studying the construction will save you more time later.

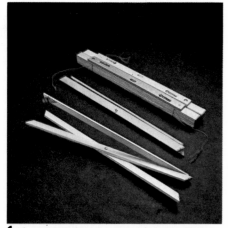

1. Leg crosspieces, cut to size, are connected by means of a ¼" carriage bolt and wingnut. Support braces are fastened with a wood screw so as to be movable.

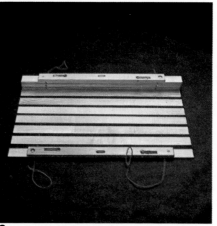

2. All tabletop boards are threaded together with a 6'6" long cord of ⅛" nylon.

3. Both mounting boards are movable. They are fastened to the outer boards of the tabletop with carriage bolts at one end. The other end rests on a peg (see next caption).

4. Mounting boards, when in lengthwise, folded position, rest on glued-in pegs. When in use, mounting boards are stabilized by pegs at right angles to tabletop boards.

5. The two pieces of cord connecting the tabletop boards to one another are tied together under the table. The table legs can then be assembled and attached.

6. To keep the table legs from slipping out of the mounting board, make a safety pin out of heavy wire and position in the slots for the legs.

7. The safety pin, fastened to the wood by a piece of string, is inserted into a hole drilled through the mounting board and table leg.

8. Once all four legs have been secured with the safety pins, the braces are installed; they are fastened by wingnut to the opposite pair of table legs.

9. Connection of the braces: The same wingnut holds the legs together and fastens the brace. Loosen wingnut, slip in the slotted bracket on the support brace, and tighten.

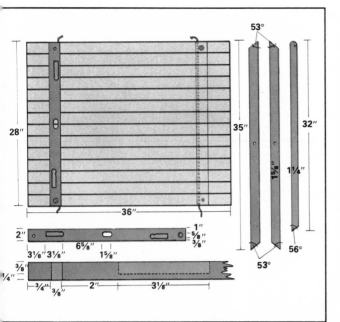

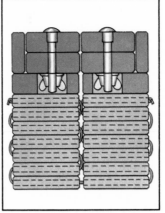

Drawing to the left shows tabletop and leg framework. The mounting board (also shown) and exact angles for cutting table legs are particularly important. The illustration above shows how the table is folded into an easy-to-carry package.

The best material for this table is Ash, which is especially elastic (used for hunting bows), but if not available you may substitute another hardwood. The boards can be cut and planed for you in a local millwork shop, or do it yourself if you have the equipment.

Construction should not prove difficult, although you must have a good drill press for the required drilling.

Great care should be used in working the tabletop mounting boards. All dimensions are shown exactly in the drawings. Be sure that slots for the table legs are not centered, but are equidistant from the center as shown. Recesses for bolts and nuts connecting mounting boards and underside of tabletop boards are ¾ in. in diameter and drilled to a depth of

MATERIAL LIST
Top: 14—2'' x ⅜'' x 36''
Mounting boards: 2—2'' x ⅝'' x 28''
Table legs: 4—1⅝'' x ⅝'' x 35''
Cross braces: 2—1¼'' x ⅜'' x 32''
2 carriage bolts: ¼'' x 2⅜''
2 wingnuts: ¼''
2 carriage bolts: ¼'' x ¾''
2 nuts: ¼''
2 screws for attaching upper ends of braces (to be countersunk)
2 hinges about 1³/₁₆'' wide, brass
13 feet of ⅛'' nylon cord

⅜ in. The recess which accommodates the crossed-leg wingnut in the table's stored position (¹³/₁₆ in. or the size of the wingnut used) goes all the way through the wood. Be sure you cut the correct angles for the legs and braces just as shown (material list includes allowances).

A lovely piece of furniture that looks fragile at first sight, but can stand up to any picnic load.

Build a barbecue this weekend

1.   A recess 55⅛" x 25⅝" is dug out to a depth of 7⅞". Fill in sand to a depth of 2", and pour concrete to the top. Even out the surface with a level, and let stand approximately 24 hours. Lay the cement slabs on top.

2.   Brick by brick, the barbecue is built up. We used dark-tinted ready-mixed mortar. This provides a pretty contrast to the white bricks. Measure and plumb exactly.

In just one weekend, and maybe two leftover holidays, your barbecue will be completed.

Massive groundwork is not required for this barbecue, since the foundation measures only 55⅛ in. x 25⅝ in. and is dug out to a depth of 7⅞ in. Selecting a good location is one of the most important requirements, because once the barbecue is standing it cannot be moved. In choosing an area, keep in mind your need for privacy, and the prevailing wind.

Stake out the four corners for the foundation with posts, and dig it out. Pour in a layer of gravel approximately 2 in. deep, and top with concrete (mixture ratio, 1:3). Smooth out the concrete; level, and let set. Cure the concrete for several days by covering with wet burlap; keep burlap wet at least 48 hours. You can probably build the foundation during the week after work. Then you will have the entire weekend to devote to the rest of the work, without having to wait for the concrete to set. Lay the two cement slabs on this foundation, and align them with the first row of bricks. When everything is aligned, proceed with the bricking. Brick for brick, the barbecue walls go up. Plumb and scale, exactly.

Fit the T-rails into the end of the wood bin so that they will overlap from about ¾

The open fire is crackling—
fun and food always go well together.

3. Two small T-rails are laid across the front of the wood bin. The face brick are put on top. Inside there should be a ⅝" ledge to hold the table boards (leave expansion room between the table boards).

in. to ⅛ in. onto the brick. Then cement on the face bricks. Place them on the wood bin in such a way that a ledge of approximately ⅝ in. is on the inside to support the table boards. After the mortar is set, clean excess off with a filling trowel.

While the mortar is drying you will have plenty of time to make the grill rack and hood. (If making the rack seems too much trouble, measure the opening and buy one.) The rack consists of steel bars (⅜ in. x ⅜ in.) and round rods (¼ in.). How many rods you put in crosswise depends on what type and size foods you usually grill. Mark the position for the rods on the square bars, center, and drill to the middle of the material. Fit the rack together and rivet the two ends. Drill two holes into the angle rails of the fire plate and grill rack. The distance to the outer edges will be ⅝ in. Make the side panels for the copper hood, using the sketch in the TIP box as a guide. The peak of the hood meets ¹¹/₁₆ in. from the front edge, and 3¹⁵/₁₆ in. above the fold. Where the side panels are to be riveted onto the hood, make a ⁷/₁₆-in. flange, and

bend the hood the same as the side panels, which will serve as a gauge.

Then rivet the hood and sides together. The distance to the outer edges is ¹⁵/₁₆ in. Once the mortar has set, drill the holes for the angle iron rails. You can see the exact position in photos 6 and 11. The pole for the hood will be held in place by

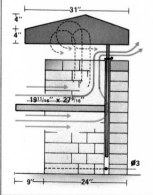

TIP

Barbecuing is fun and your guests will be delighted with the fire, but both create smoke. That is why our barbecue has an asymmetrical hood and an opening between the rear wall and the fire plate. You can see the reason why in the drawing; the smoke will not blow in your face.

4. The barbecue in the rough. The board on the left holds the tools for the grill. The board is held by flat irons which are put in during construction. The board should be made of beech, or some other wood that does not give off resin or yellow acid.

Note on U.S. Sizes: Brick shown here appears to be sand-line brick 4½" x 2⅞" x 9½". This does not match our U.S. brick sizes, which are 3⅝" x 2¼" x 7⅝" or SCR brick at 5⅝" x 2¼" x 11⅝". Locally, other sizes may be available. Quantities given are European, so adjustment must be made for U.S. quantities. Some adjustment in dimensions may be advisable to minimize brick cutting.

U.S. sand-line brick may crack under heat, so a better solution would be to build the entire barbecue from cream-color fire brick, with the exception of the red brick on top.

The patio slabs are not in U.S. Sizes. You may wish to make your own as shown on pages 26 to 29, or cast in place to whatever size is required. Another option is to lay fire brick flat in this area.

MATERIALS LIST

Sand-line brick 4½″ x 2⅞″ x 9½″	140
Red face brick	30
Patio slabs 19¹¹⁄₁₆″ x 19¹¹⁄₁₆″ x 2″	2
27⁹⁄₁₆″ x 19¹¹⁄₁₆″ x 2″	1
Pre-mix concrete	1 bag
Ready-mix mortar, approximately	3 bags
Sheet copper	
Gravel, approximately	65 lbs.
Concrete (mixture 1:3) approximately	55 lbs.
Cement, approximately	55 lbs.
Sand, approximately	160 lbs.
Mortar (anthracite), approximately	265 lbs.
Sheet copper, 36¼″ x 23″ x ¹⁄₃₂″	1 each
Sheet copper, 23″ x 6⅞″ x ¹⁄₃₂″	2 each
Copper tubing, about 26⅞′ x 1″	2 each
Copper tubing, about 26⅞′ x ¾″	2 each
Angle iron rails, length of stud, 1¼″ x ⅜″	4 each
Steel square rods, 18⅜″ x ⅜″ x ⅜″	2 each
Steel round rods, 19¼″ x ¼″	as necessary
Flat iron (anchor), 10 x 1¼″ x ¼″	2 each
Straddling dowels (for screws)	8 each
Screws, ⅝″	8 each
Rivets for racks, ¼″	4 each
Pop rivets	30 each
Wood—cutting board or butcher block 15¾″ x 3¹⁵⁄₁₆″ x ¾″	5 each
Storage board (Beech), 24″ x ⅞″ x ¾″	1 each

5. The pole for the hood is put into the corners and will be held in position by the fire plate and grill rack.

7. Attach the motor to the right of the spit. Here, in the pit, it will not be in the way. Once again, drill holes only after mortar has set.

6. The angle rails for the grill rack are secured with metal screw anchors. The fire plate rests on the wall ledges. Drill dowel holes only after the mortar has set.

8. Two grill levels: below, for more intense heat; above for everything that can't be cooked fast and must rotate slowly for extra crispness.

21

9. Sheet copper hood: cut with a hacksaw, then bend. Rivet sides and top together.

the fire plate and the hood; you can also secure the rails with metal screw anchors which have been set into the brickwork with straddling dowels.

Now the barbecue is finished. You should wait till the weekend to break it in; the mortar and cement are best left to harden for a few days before you build the first fire.

10. Set the poles into the guide bars. Set the hood on so that it is flush and tight on the left and rear walls. Mark the position of the rods on the hood. Flatten the tubes on the top and rivet on.

11. So the hood can be lowered or raised, drill two holes into the posts for adjustable positioning. Secure with a pin. The boards for the tabletop must have enough play, since they will tend to expand when damp.

Attractive outdoor lighting

Bring light to your patio, garden or lawn. With do-it-yourself lighting you can create dramatic accents, light a flower bed, or provide light for a walkway. Materials similar to those shown here are available in your hardware, home center or electrical supply store. For economical solutions to your outdoor lighting needs, simply follow the instructions on the following pages.

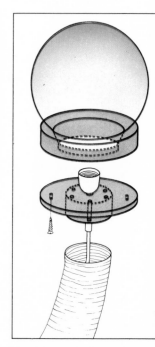

This attractive lamp consists of only a few parts. The base is an exposed aggregate patio block.

As required by the National Electrical Code, all components must be watertight and approved by Underwriters Laboratories for exterior use. The use of space-age silicone sealant will insure that everything stays dry. All edges, cable inlets or screw holes should be sealed with this compound for additional safety.

If you encounter special problems, ask your local electrical inspector or electrician for advice.

Underground cables will make the least conspicuous connections for these lighting projects, because they are specially coated and approved for underground use.

You probably already have one or more exterior outlets on your home; connect your outdoor lighting to one of these. Or, seek advice on installing an exterior outlet.

A flexible exhaust pipe of about four inches diameter, available from your local automotive supply, has been used for this lamp. An exposed aggregate patio block was used as a base. Bore through the block and attach a ¾-in. exterior grade plywood disc with a bolt. The disc should be the diameter of the inside of

your pipe.

Bore through once more for the cable inlet. Attach a ¾-in. dowel that is 24 in. long to provide additional support for the flexible pipe from the inside. The pipe is placed over the dowel and attached to the wooden disc. Seal with silicone sealant.

The globe can be fastened to a wooden ring with silicone sealant and the assembly screwed onto a plywood base.

Waterproof lights are attached to a wooden column made of ¾" boards that are 6" or more in width and 16" long. Use treated material for the wood. A top and shade of grained aluminum are attached.

The three sheets of aluminum for the shade are cut to proper size, bent and connected with pop-rivets.

These industrial lights come already waterproofed, and protected against breakage.

Inexpensive industrial lights which can be purchased at your electrical supply outlet are mounted on a wooden column. Shades of textured aluminum or fiberglass will

prevent glare. Note that connections and cable inlet must be sealed against moisture. You may paint the wooden column or apply clear finish.

Here the house number can be found in the dark. This lighted sign is protected from moisture with plastic panes.

The underground cable is hidden in the post by grooving the facing pieces of 5/4 x 5/4 or by dadoing and covering with a strip. A fluorescent fixture, approved for exterior use, is mounted in the frame.

...elf Adhesive Numbers attach to a plexiglas pane of about 12 in. x 24 in.; they are illuminated from the inside with fluorescent light. The two posts can be made of two pieces of treated 5/4 x 5/4 material 36 in. long. Two each are glued together.

A frame for mounting the fluorescent tube can be made out of exterior plywood and attached to the posts. Attach panes with chrome screws or decorative mirror tacks. Seal panes with clear silicone. Set posts about 18 in. into the ground.

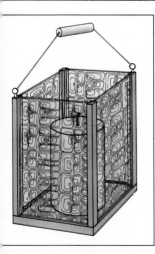

...e sides of this attractive windlight ...e colored, textured glass. You will ...d a large selection at your home ...enter. Of course, it can only be used ...summer nights with no rain.

Textured glass panes can be cut to size by a glazier, or substitute plastic panes.

Windlights are illuminated with a candle. Textured colored glass adds to the charm. For the handyman, such lamps are easy to build. The square uprights are fastened on the square solid wood base with glue and dowels once the rabbets for the glass have been

5/4" x 5/4" pine is used for the frames. The panes are held in 1/4" deep rabbets.

cut.

The panes are glued into the grooves with a clear silicone sealant. Into two opposite vertical members insert screw eyes which are connected with picture wire. A dowel with a hole drilled through its length serves as a handle.

Underground cables look like this: outer coat of rubber, inner coat of asbestos. The individual wires are also rubber coated. Some are white.

Exterior outlets in the U.S. are constructed differently than as shown. Install in compliance with the National Electrical Code.

Colorful patio blocks for garden and terrace

Every building supply dealer sells patio blocks of varying size and type, but these outdoor accents can also be made at home. Although the blocks require some time, you can save a lot of money; and the shape, color and composition of the material will be your choice.

Patio blocks for garden path and terrace do not all have to be square or rectangular. Why not sometimes round, triangular, or the shape of a cross? If you pour your own patio blocks, you can make any of these shapes, most of which are hard to find in stores.

A 20 in. x 20 in. patio block should be no less than 2½ in. thick. For 10 in. x 10 in. blocks the thickness may be reduced.

The wooden forms for the blocks are made of 2 in. x 3 in. lumber. After sawing the lumber to the desired length, the pieces are joined at all but one corner with hinges. A toggle lock is attached to the last corner. That way the form, whether triangular or square, can be closed tightly. For round blocks a simple cake mold serves well.

The folding mechanism makes it easy to open the

The frames for the patio blocks are made of 2 x 3 lumber. All corners but one are hinged. Screw a toggle lock on the last corner so that the form can be opened after the slab has been poured. Unattached wooden inserts can be used to change a square mold to an octagonal shape or the shape of a cross. All unattached pieces must have identical dimensions for uniform block size. If the blocks are not uniform, they cannot be laid in an even pattern.

Once gravel layer of an exposed aggregate block has been washed, the frame can be opened. The block has to dry four days before it can be lifted; wait three weeks before using.

You can easily make patio blocks for less than one dollar each in materials. Such patio blocks often cost more than twice as much if purchased ready-made...if you can find what you want.

1. The "building site" is prepared: spread a plastic tarp; assemble materials for exposed aggregate patio blocks...cement, gravel, wood float, trowel, oil for the form and a large paint brush.

2. Before the cement for the patio blocks is poured, the wooden form has to be generously brushed with oil so the frame can easily be removed later.

3. The base course of cement is placed into the frame about 2⅜" deep (mixture: 1 part cement, 5 parts gravel). Tamp down firmly with the trowel and smooth out.

4. For exposed aggregate the second course consists of four parts gravel, one part fine sand and one part cement. The mixture has to be somewhat moister than just damp.

5. Place this gravel cement with the trowel onto the base layer and distribute evenly. The layer should be level with the frame. Tamp slightly.

6. The layer is leveled and smoothed with the wood float. It is recommended that you wet the wood float well with water.

7. The gravel course is washed with a wet paint brush. Wet the brush repeatedly and pull across the top until the gravel is exposed.

8. Smooth patio blocks may be tinted with cement dye. Mix powdered dye with cement (1:1), dust on top, and rub into the damp cement with the wood float.

9. After the dye has been well rubbed in, the surface is smoothed thoroughly with a metal trowel. Cement dyes hold their color for many years.

With self-made frames, a great variety of shapes and types of patio blocks can be made at home.

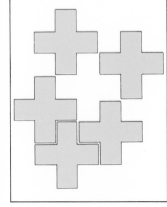

The unique cross-shaped blocks allow decorative paving of paths and patios.

mold without damaging the soft cement after tamping the cement in place.

To pour blocks, place the form on a level surface which must be covered with a plastic tarp. An appropriately large surface will be needed for pouring a large number of blocks.

Patio blocks always are poured in two courses: a base layer and a finish course.

For the base layer... which is, depending on the size of the blocks, between 2 in. - 2⅜ in. thick...

a cement mix of 1 part cement and 4 parts fine aggregate is used.

After the frames for the blocks have been oiled on the inside (repeat for each block) the damp cement can be poured and tamped into the mold.

● Smooth patio blocks:
Over the base layer apply finishing cement mixed at a ratio of 1:2 cement and sand (somewhat moister than just damp). Using a wood float, carefully level this finishing course

and screed so the cement is flush with the top of the form. Subsequently the surface should be smoothed again with the steel trowel.

● Tinting patio blocks:
Pulverized cement pigments mixed 1:1 with dry cement are dusted on the top course, rubbed in with the wood float, and subsequently smoothed.

● Aggregate blocks:
A mixture of 4 parts gravel (coarseness as desired), 1

part fine sand and 1 part cement, somewhat moister than just damp, is placed over the base layer and leveled with the wood float. The gravel is then washed with a large wet paint brush until the gravel structure shows.

After a few minutes the frame can be carefully removed from the fresh block. After about 4 days blocks can be lifted and stacked vertically. They must harden for about three more weeks before they can be used.

It is not difficult to pour garden steps. The mold is filled with cement, which has to dry for four days. Then the next step can begin.

Mold for a step. Drive the stakes into the ground to firmly support the form when the cement is poured.

Just like making patio blocks, the base layer is tamped onto a thin layer of gravel. A tamper is essential.

The course for the exposed aggregate cement is placed. The step will have to dry for at least four days before using.

Construction of the ash container is not difficult when tin-plates are fixed between the boards.

The floor plate is furnished with riveted corner pieces for the attachment of the side and ground plates.

Side and floor plates will provide additional protection so no heat can escape.

Wood stove for house and garden

Inside in winter, outside in summer: This double-walled combination fireplace and stove is easy to transport and can also be used as a grill.

If you have a spare flue on your existing chimney, this stove can easily be attached to it. Do not attempt to attach it to a flue already in use for your heating plant (for information about prefabricated and other flues, see our *Book of Successful Fireplaces,* 20th edition).

Building this fireplace-stove requires only a few special tools: sheet metal shears, pop-rivet tool, and a small welding setup that can be rented. You may wish to have a sheet metal shop cut out the metal plates according to the pattern. We also recommend having the curved pieces prebent there. This can be done by machine and shouldn't cost much, and turns out a neater job than you can achieve yourself.

ide tin-plates and assembly corners re mounted. The ash container is laced laterally with the tin-plate orners for better use.

The fire-grate: A double edge plate, with flat rail. High, curved (bent) tongues prevent slippage.

To mount the cover sheet, drill holes with 1/8" drill and attach the sheet metal sides with strong pop-rivets on the grooves (joints).

The outer (external) metal chimney and heat shield: the protective curves with two screw-clamps fixed, drilled and joined with rivets.

The chimney opening is cut from the tin-plate with a keyhole-saw to match our pattern.

The undersides of the smoke pipe are cut in 13/16" intervals and the grooves (joints) of the chimney tin-plate slope are adapted to fit. Then solidly riveted to the chimney plates.

The heat shield, which the chimney outer sides of the upper heat element should shelter, is also attached with tin plate rivets and pop-rivets.

The chimney wall is attached to the heat shield and a four-edged foot (1/4" x 1/4") is riveted to floor plates to provide even support.

A large garden tub of e posed aggregate ceme serves as a stove base. Yo may wish to use any tub terra cotta, concrete, etc as available.

Begin with the botton which contains the ashpar The bottom and the bas plate are made of 16 gaug (1/16 in.) galvanized shee metal to prevent heat warp ing. All other sheets ma be 20 gauge (1/32 in.) ga vanized.

Riveted angle plates ho all parts together. The bo tom plate is also welded This is for safety, since liv cinders and ashes drop int the ashpan. The drawer- side seams of which ar also welded—runs in tw guide rails. Allow about 3/ in. clearance on each side t allow for heat expansior The lip on the drawer fror covers this space. standard iron drawer pull riveted on the drawer fror and onto both sides t make the stove portable.

The fireplace is simp set on the base tub. It is no necessary to attach it pe manently, as the weight sufficient to hold it in place

The U.S. National Fir Protection Association re quires that the bottom the stove should be 18 ir from the floor, but this ma be reduced to four inches the area under the stove completely covered wit metal or other noncombus tible material. This stov should have a hearth pro jecting at least 18 in. in fror of the stove to catch an sparks.

Normally, stoves of thi kind are required to hav 36 in. clearance on bac and sides (distance fron combustible materials, in cluding planters or dry wall). However, with th double-wall construction o this stove, these clearance may be slightly reduce (consult *Book of Successfu Fireplaces* 20th Edition).

A metal worker can cut according to these patterns. You will still need some tin-plate strips in order to be able to make your own connecting angle. One final item is the smoke outlet: You must measure it for yourself, once you know where the chimney will stand.

53"

OUTER SHELL
INNER SHELL

16"

21 5/8"

OUTER RING   6"
8"   95"

FOUNDATION
12"
4 3/4" 15"
12"
16 1/8"

STABILIZING SHEET, PLATE
CORNER SECTION

17"
ASH COFFER
21 5/8"
15 3/8"
4 3/4"
16 1/2"
6"
1 1/2"

SCREEN, HOOD, SHADE

Build your own high-quality outdoor furniture. This table, bench and chair can easily be carried, but the group is rugged and weather-resistant.

Just Glue: Outdoor Furniture

These furniture pieces are child's play to build and to carry; they are made of plastic DWV (Drain, waste, vent) pipe—absolutely waterproof and weather-resistant. The canvas sling seats make for very comfortable seating.

Use three-inch diameter pipe. For the chair, bench and table, you should purchase five 10-ft. lengths of pipe, 25 90-degree elbows, 20 tee joints, four couplings, and some PVC solvent cement. This material is available at your home center. Your cost will be about $140.00, plus whatever you care to spend for marble, fiberglass or plywood table top. The pipe comes in two colors, white and beige. So, if one of these colors suits your decor, you need not plan on painting it.

This outdoor furniture of plastic pipe is comfortable for relaxing on the patio or lawn.

The material: 3″ plastic pipe, elbows, F joints and couplings.

The pipe is easy to saw to the desired length with a hacksaw.

Gaskets should not be needed with material used in the U.S. Be sure cement is continuous around the pipe.

Apply cement with a brush. A slight twist, and the joint is finished. Remove any excess cement at once

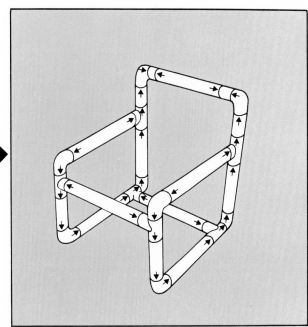

Assemble in the direction of the arrows. Dimensions, 29½" x 29½" with a back 31½" high. ▶

The bench is the same as the chair, but about 51½" wide. All dimensions can be altered as you wish. ▼

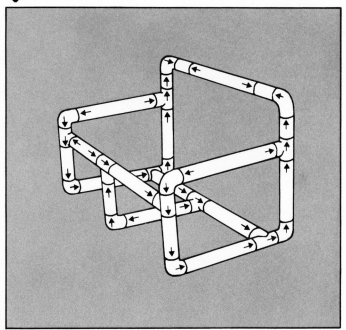

The table can be adjusted to the size of the family. Here it is built corresponding to the chair size, 29½" x 29½". Use whatever you wish as a top. Marble is shown. ▼

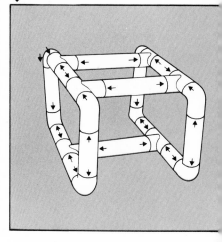

This is what the frame of the settee looks like before it is finished. After painting (if desired), only the slings need be attached to complete.

First, saw all the pipes to length with a hack saw. Preassemble to check lengths, then take apart and lay on the ground. With the type of pipe and solvent cement used in this country, you will not need the gaskets shown in the photos.

Assemble as shown in drawings, following the arrows. Apply the solvent cement with a brush, place into connector and twist slightly; setting will be almost instantaneous. Immediately wipe off any excess cement.

Should you wish to paint, use an acrylic spray; it is the easiest.

The canvas slings can now be cut and sewn. For comfort, the slings should have sufficient slack, as shown. A rustproof zipper will make them removable.

35

Build a weathercock from sheet copper

In earlier times, particularly in Europe, the weathercock was a common decoration on the tops of church and castle towers, on city halls and farm houses. Any passerby could look up to check the direction of the prevailing winds — the beak would show the wind's direction. Here we have adapted this attractive tradition to today's practical needs and decorative tastes; the bright copper reflects the sunlight.

To build your weathercock, you should first enlarge the pattern to the size you want. Whether you prefer to design your own weathercock or use one of our suggested patterns, you should first build a model using stiff paper or cardboard. This model can then be used for cutting out the sheet copper; just take your pattern along when you buy the copper. Look for suitable scraps at your hardware or lumber dealer; for the body we chose .040 in. thick sheet copper, and for head and tail, .060 in.

Using your pattern, trace the parts onto the sheet copper, using a felt pen. Cutting can be done with tinsnips or a sabre saw (coping saw). For the comb we strongly recommend using a saw.

If you bend the mate-

After tracing the contours of the parts onto the sheet copper, carefully cut each section.

The detailed areas of the head and the tail can be cut with a sabre saw or a coping saw.

After cutting all the pieces, use a file to remove the burrs and then polish with emery cloth.

To bend the metal for the body, clamp it between two boards. For a more accurate bend, position a steel straightedge, at the fold.

Use a flat nose pliers to bend over the flaps that will be soldered onto the other half of the body.

Slit the end of the axle pipe. Insert a steel ball bearing in the upper end and solder it in. Later on, the copper pipe will be slipped over the stainless steel axle, which is welded onto the roof ridge support.

The cut-out head is attached to the axle with solder. Bend the tail around the axle pipe and solder.

The half of the rooster body that premounted and has the tabs ar belly must be soldered onto the sha that also connects the head and ta Just spot-solder at head, legs and ta and adjust.

Once the body has been completed, the feet should be soldered blunt-edged onto the axle pipe that is sticking out of the belly. Attach the feet on one side at a time.

Shown are the cross-arms for the four points of the compass, which are also of copper pipe. Flatten the pipe centers and solder together. Drill the hole for the axle in the center. Bend tabs onto each of the four ends, where the letters will be attached.

Mounting the weathercock to the roof requires a support shaped like you roof ridge. This support carries your rotating axle with cross an weathercock, and should be attached to the top of your roof ridg

rial while cutting, flatten it out with a rubber or wooden hammer. There is a chance that the sheet copper will work-harden if you hammer it too much. This can be corrected by heating it with a torch and letting it slowly cool.

The weathercock rotates on top of a stainless steel rod that is inside a copper pipe and welded to a roof gable support. These moving parts have to be adjusted so they will turn freely without excessive play. A steel ball sitting at the end of the pipe is the actual bearing (which may be taken out of an old car or bought at a bicycle shop). Bend one side of the body and belly, fit carefully to the rod, and solder. Align other half of body and belly, straightening out the tabs so they touch each other on their edge faces. Solder the two halves first on the tabs, then close the open seams. (Copper loses heat so fast that it is not advisable to use a hard solder.) Solder the feet to the pipe; file off any burrs; sand and polish the bird. To keep the weathercock bright and shiny, cover it with a coat of clear varnish.

Cut out the letters N, W, S, E and solder them onto the copper cross; then solder the cross to the support. To locate the letter N, use the help of a good reliable compass.

Because copper is nearly indestructible, you should have many years of enjoyment watching your weathercock turn on the roof.

You will enjoy your project even more when you design your own weathervane. Here are our suggestions:

1) Contemporary weathercock
2) Sailor looking through spyglass
3) Weathercock — Gallic design

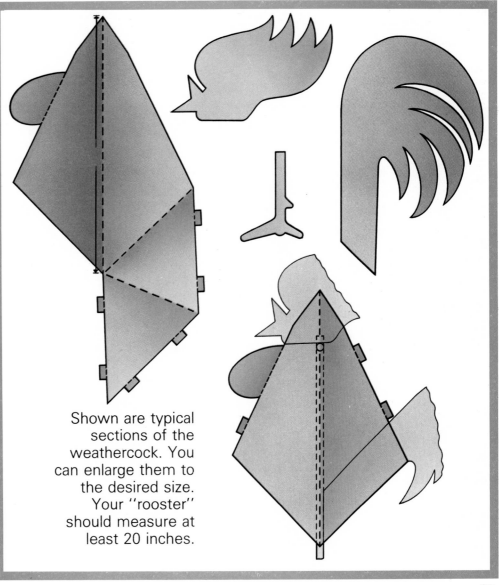

Shown are typical sections of the weathercock. You can enlarge them to the desired size. Your "rooster" should measure at least 20 inches.

Collapsible Hollywood swing

This Hollywood swing is large enough for one to comfortably stretch out, or offers easy seating for two. The blue/green striped canvas is sold for awnings, but is very suitable for this purpose.

The detachable connections consist of T-nuts or "Tap It" Nylon inserts.

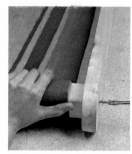

After the canvas has been attached, the canopy frame is screwed together.

Sew each canvas seam sufficiently wide to allow for the insertion of a batten strip, which is screwed to the wood rail. This holds canvas under weight.

Bronze shackles serve as loops at the end of the chain that is placed over the frame ends.

For this swing, we recommend either Douglas Fir or Yellow Pine, fairly clear, and your choice of canvas.

All parts can be quickly assembled using screws of the type shown in the illustration — a sleeve with coarse thread on the outside and a standard machine screw thread on the inside. If you have difficulty finding these screws, you may use as a substitute either T-nuts, "Tap It" Nylon inserts, or alternate types recommended by your local hardware outlet.

Note: It is possible to use 2 in. x 4 in. nominal instead of the $^5/_4$ in., but then the lengths of all horizontal members must be increased accordingly (check the actual sizes of the wood you buy in order to make adjustments.)

The machine screw, screwed through the first leg into the sleeve in the mortised end of the horizontal rail, holds everything together.

The rear leg carries most of the weight of the swing because the mortised end has been fastened only in that section.

Placing the canopy on top and attaching it is the last job. Once the canopy has been adjusted, the canvas can be pulled tight by turning the cross-rails.

First round the wide parts of the frame at all ends using a keyhole or jig saw to cut the semi-circle; finish with a rasp, and sand. The legs are rounded only at the top; at the bottom they are cut on a slant to fit closely to the ground.

Drill one 1¼ in. hole in the centers of each of the circles at the tops of the two inner legs. This will receive the round mortised end of the upper rail.

The side braces, which keep the legs from spreading, are now attached. It would be best to use sleeved fasteners as shown, or a T-nut, because bolting through may catch and tear the clothing of the user. A long wood screw can be used, but then the swing will not collapse as readily. When drilling, mark where the sleeve will be inserted.

Now mark and cut the mortised ends of the top rail, using a saw and a

chisel. Finish with a rasp. The mortise cut is made to the length and depth of the stock you are using. The pictures here show 1¼ in. ($^5/_4$ in.) stock but 2 in. x 4 in. may be more readily available, and will work as well. Put mortised ends into the inner legs; place outer round of leg on top and drill through. Turn sleeve for the screw into the mortised end.

Screw the canvas for the swing to the horizontal rails by inserting lattice into the seam and screwing lattice to rails. For the ends of the rails make loops in the chain with the aid of shackles (chain links that can be opened). Place loops over the frame. Now you can attach swing side members to swing rails using wood screws. To prevent the rails from turning under the load, they are doweled at the end on each side with ⅜ in. dowels. The chain for the swing is held on the top rail

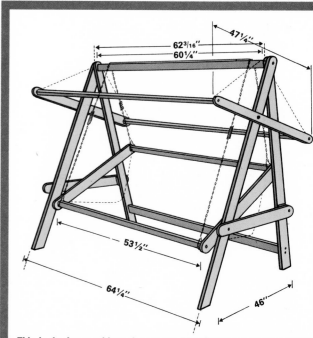

This is the frame without the canvas. The Hollywood swing consists of three parts: basic stand, hanging swing, and canopy. All parts are built separately and then assembled. Note: Dimensions are approximate.

Note: Do not substitute 2" x 2" nominal (1½ in. x 1½ in. actual) for rails on the canopy and swing; it may not be rigid enough.

To compensate for the spacing between the legs, the rear end of the cross-piece has been reinforced with a piece of lumber.

Springs prevent a too-sudden load on the chain and ensure soft operation of the swing.

MATERIALS

Canopy Stand
2 sides $^5/4''$ x 4'' x $47^1/4''$
*2 cross rails
$1^7/8''$ x $1^7/8''$ x $64^{11}/32''$
2 lattice (approx.)
$^1/8''$ or $^3/16''$ x $1^1/2''$ x $59^1/16''$

Swing
2 sides $^5/4''$ x 4'' x $41^{11}/32''$
*2 cross rails
$1^7/8''$ x $1^7/8''$ x $53^{17}/32''$
2 lattice (approx.)
$^1/8''$ or $^3/16''$ x $1^1/2''$ x $51^3/16''$.

Canvas finish sizes
Canopy $68^{29}/32''$ x $59^1/16''$
Swing $64^{31}/32''$ x $51^3/16''$
2 cushions $45^9/32''$ x $25^{19}/32''$
Foam padding for
2 cushions $44^7/8''$ x $25^7/32''$

Miscellaneous:
2 chains $78^3/4''$
8 coupling links
4 shackles (hardware or
marine supply)
4 tension springs
16 special fasteners, 2''
4 special fasteners, $3^3/16''$
(Use "T-nuts" or "Tap It"
Nylon Inserts)

with a screw.

After the swing has been assembled, attach the back cross-brace with 2 screws at each leg.

Fasten the canopy: the sleeved fastener or T-nut holding the canopy at the sides must be tightened just enough so that the canopy can be adjusted but not tilted too easily. Now the top rail can be fastened with screw, T-nut, or nylon insert; here also, a dowel next to the screw can keep the rail from rotating.

To get a free-swinging effect, insert tension springs in the chain as shown, with the aid of coupling links.

Be sure that all edges are well rounded. Finish all parts with several coats of sealer and a clear preservative.

At the top rail, attach chain by a link-thickness with a screw. Add a shim to keep the canvas from chafing against the chain.

In a properly equipped aviary the birds will find protection, companionship, and adequate living space.

A Beautiful Cage for Your Feathered Friends

An aviary is an attractive focal point in a summer garden, on the patio, or on a balcony.

This outdoor bird cage consists of three individual units attached with wing nuts. Construction of the individual units is based on the hexagon, with six sides of equal length. The three front sides are enclosed with ½-in. hardware cloth; the three rear sides are enclosed with glass. The aviary should be placed with glass facing toward the prevailing wind. The roof consists of three ⁵/₁₆" plywood panels, screwed to a deck underneath.

The center section of the aviary deviates slightly from the basic construction (base and cover of ⁵/₁₆-in. plywood). Here an enclosed nesting box offers shelter to its residents. The front of this nesting box consists of

1. The bases for the dowels are recessed by ¹/₁₆" with the wood bit; predrill screw holes.

2. The round or half-round dowels are screwed and glued to the plywood panels.

3. The hardware cloth, needed to cover the sides at the front, is cut to proper size with wire cutters.

Our aviary is "portable." assembled as three individual u and can be easily taken do During the cold season it quickly be moved to a bright, hea room indoors and reassembled th

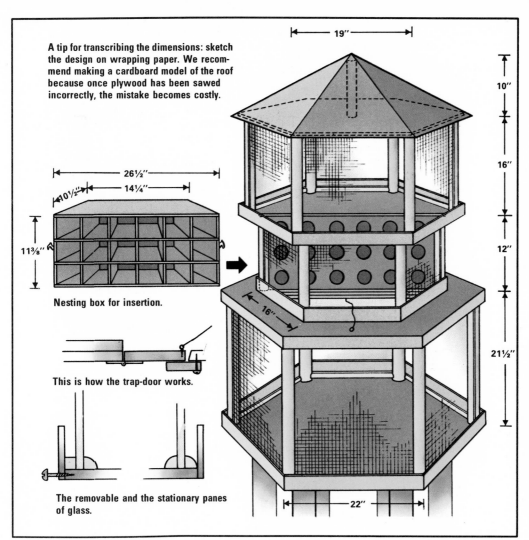

A tip for transcribing the dimensions: sketch the design on wrapping paper. We recommend making a cardboard model of the roof because once plywood has been sawed incorrectly, the mistake becomes costly.

19"

10"

16"

12"

21½"

26½"

14¼"

10½"

11⅜"

Nesting box for insertion.

16"

22"

This is how the trap-door works.

The removable and the stationary panes of glass.

4. The hardware cloth is stapled to the halved dowels on the outside It must be stretched tight!

5. The second half of the dowel tapped in with a hammer. Three screws hold both strips together.

6. The wire mesh is framed on both sides (top and also bottom) by quarter molding nailed in place.

7. Glass panes are installed to the weather side of the aviary. They are held in place by quarter molding at top and bottom only. At the sides they rest flush against the dowels. (Measure accurately; this is best done after the unit has been assembled.)

8. After wire-mesh and panes are in place, the facing strip is glued and nailed in place (1" x 2").

a permanently installed board, into which round access holes have been drilled with a wood bit. The rear section, subdivided into small boxes that offer "nest-warmth" to the birds, is removable. This compartmented unit is attached to the front with two hooks. The size and number of these nesting boxes used will depend on the occupants of the aviary. Prior to construction, consult a pet shop, library, the local Humane Society, or see page 85 of *Successful Pet Homes* by Larry Mueller.

The top and bottom of the center unit, bottom of the top unit, and top of the bottom unit are provided with an opening cut-out that allows the birds unim-

peded access to all three levels of the aviary. Therefore, all that remains in the front of the base and cover of the center unit is a frame of 2⁹/₁₆-in. width, to which dowels and hardware cloth are attached. Clearance:

MATERIALS
Plywood: Exterior—2 good sides preservative-treated. ½"—2 sheets 4' x 8'; ⁵/₁₆"—1 sheet 4' x 8' ⅛"—1 sheet 4' x 8'
Round stock: Legs—use 20 lineal feet of peeled cedar fence post about 3" in diameter.
Columns—use about 27 lineal feet largest dowel or closet pole obtainable—1" ±.
Quarter Round—¾", about 100'; ½" x 2" actual, 27'; (or use 1" x 2" nominal); ½" galvanized wire mesh (hardware cloth); *3 panes of glass about 21½" x 19"; *3 panes of glass about 16" x 17";
Hardware: brass screws, galvanized nails; 27½" piano hinge, 1 magnetic catch.
*Measure for exact size

front edge 13½ in. long; rear edge 26⅜ in. long; both are 11⅛ in. deep. The openings, which have to be cut into the bottom of the top unit and into the top of the bottom unit (both ½-in. plywood), correspond to these dimensions.

For easy cleaning of the aviary you need the largest possible access openings to the individual cages. The piece of plywood which is cut out of the top of the bottom unit was installed as a trap-door. This trap-door attaches with piano hinge to the long edge, and is held against the ceiling of the lower level with a magnetic catch when not in use. It is disengaged by a pull-chain and closed at the front with a safety bolt as needed.

9. Nesting boxes are in the center of the aviary. The box is inserted behind the access holes and held in place by hooks.

10. The roof construction: a screw-attached dowel supports the six roof sections, which are screwed to the deck underneath.

11. The assembly: Ram the support posts about 12" deep into the ground, then attach the bottom unit with 4" wood screws. The remaining units are attached with threaded bolts (¼" x 1¼") and wing nuts.

All levels have a small hatch in the hardware cloth, the overlapping flap is cut of galvanized hardware cloth and closed with a wooden peg) so that birds can be brought into the desired cage during clean-up.

Now the center glass-pane, the molding for which is glued to a square strip ½ in. x ½ in. and attached to the bottom with wood screws, can be removed (see drawing).

All wooden components should be finished with three coats of spar varnish to ensure you will enjoy your aviary for a long time to come.

Get an early start with a hotbed

Enthusiastic gardeners can hardly wait until they can prepare their gardens in the spring. This can be done without worry using a hotbed box, because the frost will not cross up your plans. It will give you pleasure to see your seedlings grow and know they are protected.

When does spring begin? This depends on where you live; your gardener's handbook will tell you the date of the last frost. (Check *Successful Landscaping* for dates.) Once the frost is out of the ground, you can get a head start by using a hotbed. Seedlings are raised in the box and are taken out when all danger of frost is past.

If you do not have a hotbed box, you can build one quickly and easily.

First, the basic box. You can take the dimensions from the drawing and enlarge them as you like. Either two tongue-and-groove boards (shown in drawing) or one wide board (substituted in material list) should be used for each side: sides are screwed onto the corner posts.

The intriguing "convertible top" of the hotbed is the most important part. The "trick" is in the wooden

As a cover, we have used a reinforced plastic film which filters the ultraviolet rays.

48

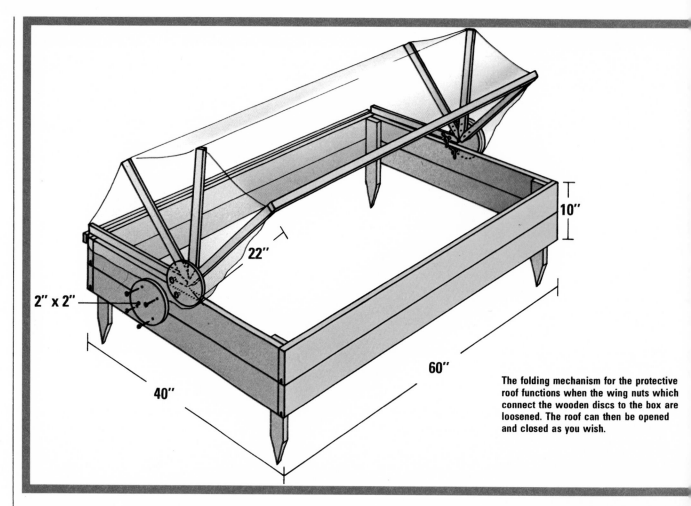

2" x 2"

22"

10"

40"

60"

The folding mechanism for the protective roof functions when the wing nuts which connect the wooden discs to the box are loosened. The roof can then be opened and closed as you wish.

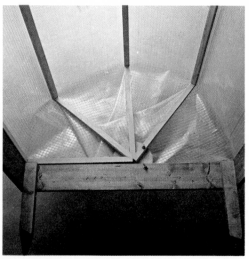

The plastic sheet is fastened to each side by placing it onto the first wooden disc and then applying another disc on top with screws (see above). The roof frame consists of four pieces of 1" x 2" which are fastened to the inside wood disc.

disc that is connected to the frame. It functions like a cam.

The vertical roof supports should be cut to points at one end so that the pointed ends will rest in the center of the disc. The horizontal supports are glued and nailed to the verticals. Three of these four frame racks are fastened securely to the wooden

discs with screws. The fourth member at the rear is fastened with wing nuts and bolts.

The wooden discs which carry the frame are fastened to the base with one ¼ in. wing nut and bolt each. To do this drill one ¼ in. hole, from the inside about 27 in. from the rear and 1 in. from the top, and through the wooden disc on

MATERIAL LIST

4   ½" exterior grade plywood discs, 6" dia.
35 linear ft. of 1" x 2" pine or fir for roof frames and prop
2 ea. ¼" x 2" wing nuts and bolts
2 ea. ½" x 2½" wing nuts and bolts
2 boards, 60" ea.
22 pieces 1" x 10"—60" ea., for box, preferably treated material
23 boards 1" x 10"—40" ea.
4 corner stakes—2" x 2" x 16"
1 reinforced plastic sheet 88" x 80"

each side. The plastic sheet can now be pulled over the frame and fastened to the two end frames with another piece of 1 in. x 2 in. as a batten. Also, the outside plywood discs are applied at this time.

Finally, cut a prop to hold the frame open when working in it. This should be bolted to the base with a ¼ in. bolt.

Materials: Pine, 2" x 2". Smaller sizes can also be used.

Drill holes exactly in middle of each branch so branches will stack properly. Use vise and drillpress, if available.

Use a center notch to overlap the crossstand; the tree needs a sturdy stand.

This picture shows the structure before branches have been rotated to give a circular effect. Starting from the bottom, the branches become shorter every three layers. The starting length of the first three branches is 40", the next three branches are 36", etc.

A christmas tree forever

Easy to build, this tree will last many years. After the holidays it can be taken apart and stored in a small area. Although expensive-looking, it can be built at little cost.

For this almost-ever-lasting lighted Christmas tree, we chose 2 in. x 2 in. pine. The branches become shorter from bottom to top; 4 in. is taken off every third branch, going from 40 in. down to 8 in. Of course, you can build your tree smaller or larger according to your taste and space availability. For this tree we used pine, but for smaller trees some other woods could be used.

Assembly is quite easy. Drill a hole in a crosslike stand and mount a broomstick tightly into it. Then simply slide the branches over the stick (after drilling a hole in the center of each branch). Insert a spacer between your crossstand and your first branch to improve the optical effect. For fire safety, place it outside on your patio or in a fireproof room.

Build an adjustable sun lounge

Better made than any you can buy, this lounge can be easily moved from sun to shade, like a wheelbarrow. The detachable backrest permits you to sit up for reading, recline for dozing, or stretch out for sunbathing.

You can sit up or lie flat on your back, or do like this young lady and enjoy the sun in semi-reclining position.

The lounge shown here is made of a pine frame with spruce boards. But you may wish to use Vertical Grain Redwood or Wolmanized lumber of any species to withstand weathering. For the sides and ends, we suggest 5/4 in. (1⅛ in. material), 4¾ in. or wider. The side pieces are 79 in. long and the end dimensions are 31½ in. The top requires 16 pieces of 1 x 4 each 31½ in. long, and one 1 x 2, 31½ in. long. The backrest requires three more 1 x 4s of 31½ in. each, plus four 1 x 4s, each 26 in.

We recommend 2 x 4 x 12 in. for the legs, with the 3½ in. face grooved for the wheels.

The backrest can be securely set at a 45° or 85° angle; or you may remove that section and store it underneath. This comfortable piece of garden furniture is uncomplicated and easy to build; you may wish to create several while you are at it. All parts are glued and screwed together, and a foam pad, with a waterproof covering, can easily be made to suit.

The guides for the

backrest can also be sawn out of the 2 x 3. The wheels should be available at your hardware or do-it-yourself store.

Handles for easy movement are cut out of the last 8 in. of each side with your jigsaw. The frame sides and ends are then mortised together (photo 2). Glue together with white glue.

The guides for the backrest are glued and screwed (galvanized screws) to the two sides about 16 in. from the headboard (photo 3). One 1 x 2 x

31½ in. chamfered to the angles of the guides for the backrest, is installed above the guides (photo 6).

Now the backrest can be assembled. The ends of the boards are routed out ¼ in. x ¼ in. on both faces with a corresponding grove cut into the edges of the frame (photo 5). The last of the boards should end 4¾ in. from the end of the sides. All parts are glued together.

When not in use, the back rest can be stored under the cot with an elastic cord holding it in place (photo 7).

1. All boards should be dry, and be either redwood or treated. The two wheels with rubber tread can be bought in toy shops or special hobby shops.

2. After the handles have been sawn with the jig saw, the frame components are mortised together and glued with white glue. The edges are slightly eased.

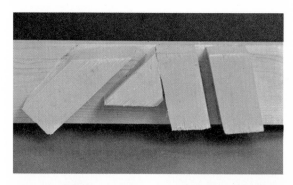

3. The guides for the backrest are cut out of 2 x 3 lumber. For a sloping position the blocks should be glued at a 45° angle, for sitting position at an 85° angle. The first guide block is glued onto the frame about 16" from the head of the cot.

4. Slot the legs to receive the wheels and round off the bottom. Attach wheels with carriage bolts large enough to fit the wheels.

5. The ends of the boards for the backrest are routed out ¼" x ¼" on each face and then a corresponding groove is cut into the inner edge of the sides.

6. A board is glued above the backrest guides, which must be chamfered corresponding to the angle of the guide. This board should also be secured with rustproof screws.

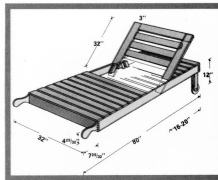

MATERIALS
Frame:
2   $^5/_4$'' x 5'' x 79''
2   $^5/_4$'' x 5'' x 31½''

Boards:
19 1 x 4 x 31½''
4   1 x 4 x 26''
1   1 x 2 x 31½''

Miscellaneous:
4   feet of 2 x 3
2   wheels
2   carriage bolts for
    axles
1   elastic cord
rustproof screws
white glue

7. The backrest is held securely in place with an elastic cord which may come from a car-top luggage holder.

8. Two wooden blocks, behind which the backrest can be stored, are glued to the two legs.

55

For climbing A jungle gym

Children can really get a workout on this backyard fort built of ordinary lumber. It has everything: climbing rope, swing, horizontal bars at different heights, and even a soccer goal. A ladder leads to the "fort" section. An ideal play gym, it is easy to build and can be erected in only a few hours.

Start assembling: At left, the post which is set into the ground. A tenon has been cut at one end, to which the two verticals are attached with threaded bolts and nuts. The tenon is of the same thickness as the vertical member.

After one side has been assembled, the short posts for the railing and the railing boards can be screwed on.

Ideal for hard play. Even when a crowd of neighborhood children comes running, this structure can withstand the assault.

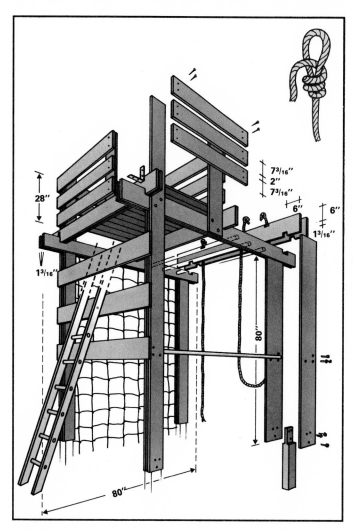

28″

7³/₁₆″
2″
7³/₁₆″
6″
6″
1³/₁₆″

1³/₁₆″

80″

80″

To give the structure added support, rocks are placed next to the posts. Fill the hole with dirt, water, and after a while tamp thoroughly.

The structure can be built of standard 2 x 6 or 2 x 8 lumber. If treated lumber is available, use it. Lumber treated with either pentachlorophenol (PCP) or Wolmanized is satisfactory. Creosoted material is not; it will dirty clothing. Even if you do not use treated material for the superstructure, it is important to use it for the foundation pieces.

Within a few hours, the entire structure can be prepared for erection.

Preliminary Work

The foundation posts should be about 36 in. long, notched to receive the uprights about 10 in. from the end. Use either 4 x 6 or 4 x 8 for these, depending on what you are using for the superstructure.

The eight pieces holding the verticals together, as ring beams, are notched 1¼ in. deep by 4½ in. wide to receive lumber (check lumber thickness), 6 in. from the ends. Drill the four pieces for the horizontal bars. Drill through the two inside pieces and halfway through the outer members. These pieces also need to be notched for the piece that carries one end of the floor boards. These members are attached by lag screws between and inside of the verticals.

The other four are bolted together with blocking in between to form two crossbeams.

Into the ladder sides drill 1 in. holes 8 in. apart. Cut small wedges out of the ends of the rungs, about 1½ in. long, to form notches. Glue and nail the rungs into position and then drive somewhat larger wedges into the notches to lock the rungs into position.

If you are using untreated lumber, you may wish to brush on two coats of preservative at this point.

Erection

Connect the verticals to the foundation pieces, which are set about 24 in. into the ground. Of course, make sure that the foundation posts are level with each other.

At 6 ft. 6 in. height, attach the horizontal ring beams with lag screws. The notches must be to the outside of the vertical pieces (see drawing).

The short posts for the railing and the railing itself are attached with screws. Assemble the other side the same way.

Use metal framing clips to attach the ring beams to each other. Screw or nail floor boards to the beams. Reinforce the post at the left of the railing with a piece of scrap lumber.

Fold net at the edges over strips which are inserted between verticals and secured with screws. Attach lower horizontal bar with three carriage bolts at

Materials

(Use 2 x 6 or 2 x 8 unless otherwise indicated).

Vertical Posts
6   8′0″—cut to 86″
2   10′0″—cut to 118″

Horizontal Ring Beams
9   8′0″—cut to 79″

Commando Tower
3   pieces 40″
3   pieces 72″
3   1 x 6 or 1 x 8   50″
1″ floor boards about 32¼″ long to cover 67″

Ladder
2   2 x 4   106½″
11   hardwood dowels for rungs 1″ x 16″

Miscellaneous
4   foundation posts 4 x 6 or 4 x 8—36″
3   climbing boards 70″
1   horizontal bar 60″ long
1″ hardwood dowel or pipe
3   horizontal bars 6′6″ long
26 feet of ¾″ rope
1   soccer net about 4′8″ x 7′3″
4   framing clips
Bolts, nails, screws and glue

each end. Protruding ends of the bolts should be sawn off and filed smooth for safety.

The rope ends should have double knots (see drawing). Pull the rope end through the loop and tighten.

The ladder is stuck into the ground and fastened at the top to the protruding end of the ring beam with three screws.

Finish by fastening the three horizontal boards on the ladder side with screws.

This is the joint for the parallel beams: in a type of sandwich construction the vertical members are screwed to the horizontal boards. The parallel beam is held by an angle bracket attached with screws.

To prevent climbing rope and swing from sliding, a notch is sawed into the parallel rails. Nail a piece of scrap lumber between the knots of the swing-rope to prevent it from pulling out.

The climbing structure is finished. The three boards on the ladder side are also for climbing, and help stabilize the structure.

The floor boards are nailed to a crossboard and the outer parallel rail. Countersink nails to prevent injuries!

A terrarium

For all plant lovers

The basic material, ready to assemble: The leg posts are grooved; horizontal and vertical bars have fitting grooves and dowels; threaded bolts and nuts provide quick assembly.

This beautiful terrarium can be left outdoors without fear of weather damage. The picture shows teak used for the wooden frame, but any quality hardwood will do. The frame is held together with wooden dowel pins, combined with threaded bolts and nuts. Everything can be easily assembled, and disassembled. Because this terrarium isn't glued together, but is built with threaded-bolts, the glass panes are easy to replace if broken and the whole framework can be knocked down to allow easy storage in a small space.

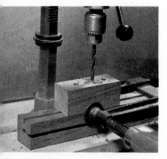

Prepare leg posts on a circular saw or router. Grooves should be about ⅛" wide, and ¼" deep. Use a template made of wood scraps to drill dowel holes and screw holes.

To drill all posts, attach a ⅜"-thick board with distances marked to indicate where holes should be drilled. Marking ensures that holes are put exactly in the middle of the material.

Two inches from outer edges of the corner posts, cut a slit equal to the width of the nut; drill a hole in the end of each corner board, pierce again, insert nut for the threaded bolt.

Drill corner connections so that the threaded bolts cross each other, offset by ⅜".

The glass plates for the terrarium are easily cut with a glass cutter; be sure to use an absolutely flat working surface.

Insert glass plates first into the grooves of the corner posts; then upper cross bars and the lower bars are fastened with dowels.

MATERIALS LIST

No.	Part	Pieces	Material	Size inches (nominal unless otherwise specified)
1	Legs	4	hardwood	21⅝", 2" x 2"
2	Lower cross bars	2	hardwood	31½", 1" x 4"
3	Lower cross bars	2	hardwood	19¾", 1" x 4"
4	Upper cross bars	2	hardwood	31½", 1" x 2"
5	Upper cross bars	2	hardwood	19¾", 1" x 2"
6	Bottom support rails	2	hardwood	32¼", 5/4" x 5/4"
7	Bottom support rails	2	hardwood	18⅞", 5/4" x 5/4"
8	Bottom cleat	2	hardwood	19¹¹/₁₆", ⅝" x ⅜" (dressed size)
9	Bottom	1	watertight plywood	31½", 20½" x ½" (dressed size)
10	Dowels	24	Beech	1⅝" x ⅜"
11	Machine screws	16		4" x 2⅜"
12	Glass plates	2		32⅝" x 14⁷/₁₆" x ⅛"
13	Glass plates	2		20⅝" x 14⁷/₁₆" x ⅛"
14	Casters	4		
15	Counterbore screws for photos 6 & 7	14		1" long

Measurements are valid for slot depths of 3⅛" - 3½"

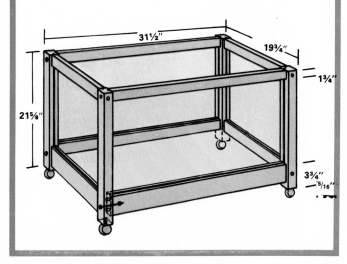

The diagram pictured below the materials list shows how the dowel and bolt holes will fit on all parts. We fastened this pattern onto the work with screw clamps and marked the drill holes by touching them lightly with the drill. Then we removed the pattern and finished drilling them on a drilling stand. To make our terrarium portable, we attached furniture casters. Use waterproof plywood for the bottom to avoid rot from the dampness.

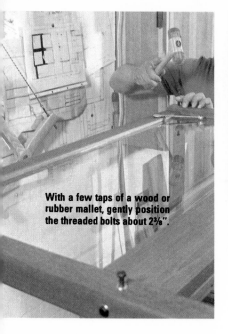

With a few taps of a wood or rubber mallet, gently position the threaded bolts about 2⅜".

▲ Insert nuts into the prepared slits. Once the bolts are tightened with an appropriate box-end or open-end wrench, the frame is complete.

The bottom plate is inserted with cleats, thus saving mortise work. ▶

Casting your own stones

Molding your own stones is fun, and can help save expenses. What is required? All you'll need are assorted molds, gravel, cement and water. Ingredients are mixed in proper proportion, poured into the mold, and a decorative stone is the result. Those who do not like dull gray can color the stones according to their own personal taste. The following tricks and devices will help make the work even more successful.

Concrete for pouring decorative stones must be neither too wet nor too dry. It would be too bad if, after drying, they were to break or become crooked and misshapen. Use four parts gravel and one part cement; stir this up with water to make the mixture "moist as soil." If you wish to add color, cement dyes are available in a wide range of shades. However, you should write down the exact mixing proportions when staining stones so that there will be no color deviation later on. Oiling the forms will help, but is not absolutely necessary.

The working principle is similar for all the molds. The metal ejection plate is

Using this mold, 8 bricks may be cast in one piece: dimensions 18" x 9" x 3½". An enclosure wall may be built quickly and without problems, or an ugly wall be covered up. Shown is a trial line-up of bricks, without foundation and mortar.

placed into the mold; the concrete mix is poured and smoothed with a trowel board. The filled mold is turned over, the ejection plate pressed down with both thumbs, and the mold is lifted off. Finally, the metal ejection plate is lifted off. Special attention must be given to filling the mold by working in layers. First

pour in one-third, tamping it well, and continue in layers, until the mold is filled. The more the concrete is packed by tamping, the more solid the stone will be. You can buy molds for a relatively low price, or build your own (see pp. 69-70 of *Practical and Decorative Concrete* by Robert Wilde). To cure stones, cover with

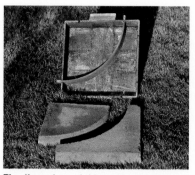

The dimensions of this mold are 11⅜″ x 11⅜″ x 2⅜″. Quarter rounds, cross, or cross-shaped stones may be produced by inserting blocks and strips. Half-size tiles may be obtained by cutting stone in half lengthwise, using the metal ejection plate after unmolding. Basic mix: Four parts gravel and one part cement are stirred up with water until "moist as soil." Photo at right shows result when too much water is used.

Cross-shaped tiles are not only decorative, but also are excellently suited for heavy-traffic areas. Using an appropriate foundation, they are just right for a garage driveway. Place the blocks into corners of the basic mold to achieve the cross shape.

wet burlap for 2 to 3 days then allow to harden at lea one week.

Stones of washed co crete are also very decor tive. Four parts river-be gravel, one part fine san and one part cement a poured into the mold a depth of approximate 1¼ in. This mixture shou be somewhat moister tha the normal concrete mix Thereafter, continue t build up stone in layers an tamp well. After unmolding

This is practical and looks good: A decorative stone edging for pathways, terraces or beds. Dimensions are approximately 18″ x 9″ x 3½″. The picture above shows the tools needed: smoothing board, stamper, and bricklayer's trowel.

MATERIAL

Face-brick mold, approx. 18″ x 9″ x 3½″; edge mold approx. 18″ x 6″ x 2⅜″; floor tile mold, approx. length of each side 11⅜″, depth 2″. Combination mold, approx. 19″ x 19″ x 2⅜″; concrete mix 4:1; riverbed gravel for washed concrete.

the stone should set for few hours. Then, using wet, soft painter's brush carefully wash out cemen left between the gravel Allow 2 to 3 days of curing and another few days fo stones to harden suffi ciently before placing int the foundation. Stones fo heavy traffic areas (for in stance garage driveway should be allowed to hard en longer, because con crete will reach its fina hardness only after three t four weeks.

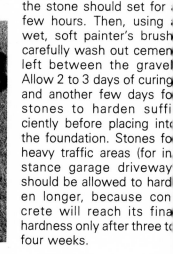

The honey-comb mold has a length of approximately 11⅜″ per side and is 2″ deep. Here, one can readily recognize the press-holes in the mold and the metal plate. This enables you to push the stone neatly from the mold. The plate guarantees a smooth surface.

Build a wooden fleet for your youngster

When children play, their toys must be able to stand rough play. The material for these projects is sturdy and inexpensive, and the fun of creating them costs little other than a few hours of your time.

We suggest toys of different sizes: a dump truck, a garage with a tractor, and two rack wagons. The material you need is plywood and sticks. Whatever models you choose, they will provide your children fun and creativity for a long time.

The Dumptruck

This toy's size—with a length of 20 in. —makes it unique compared to other similar vehicles. It also has a range of handy extras: it can be steered by a steering wheel that is attached to the top of the driver's cab; the dump-bed is tiltable; the tailgate of the dump may also be tilted upwards.

Having cut all sticks and plywood parts according to the sketch, it is best to start by gluing the chassis. Glue only the center cross sticks (see sketch). The rear stick, together with the 7¼ in.-wide plywood piece, is your tilting unit for the loading area. The two chassis beams will take a ⅜ in. hole about ⅝ in. away from the rear. Insert the dowels into the tilting unit and the chassis beams, and glue into the beams. The same principle is used for mounting the tailgate.

Before gluing the driver's cab, drill the holes for the steering column. The steering column, a ⅜ in. wood dowel, is glued to the front axle. Insert the column from underneath, through chassis and cab, and attach a 2¼ in. plywood steering wheel.

Install wheels on axles using wood screws. You can buy the wheels or make them yourself.

The Garage

Start out with the garage floor. It has to slope about 1¾ in. so the tractor and wagon can be easily driven in. Then glue on the sidewalls. The upper crossbeam (plate) is next. Drill the ⁵⁄₃₂ in. holes for the door hinge dowels into crossbeams and garage floor before attaching doors to the sidewalls. Drill same size holes in garage floor. Glue dowels in garage doors and let them stick out ⁵⁄₁₆ in. on top and bottom.

This garage has enough space for a sturdy tractor and two rack wagons. Small dowel hinges enable the doors to swing.

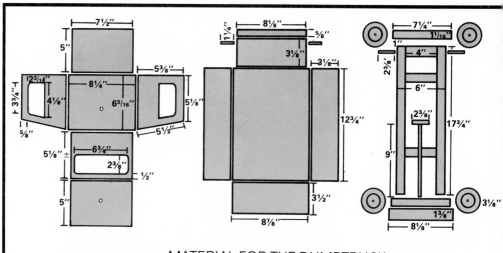

MATERIAL FOR THE DUMPTRUCK
⅜'' plywood, about 8 feet square
⅜'' dowel, about 16''
1'' square sticks, about 60''
1⅛'' or 1¼'' square sticks, about 20''
Wood or plastic wheels, 3''-3¼'', 4 pieces
Wood screws, about 1¾'', 4 pieces

66

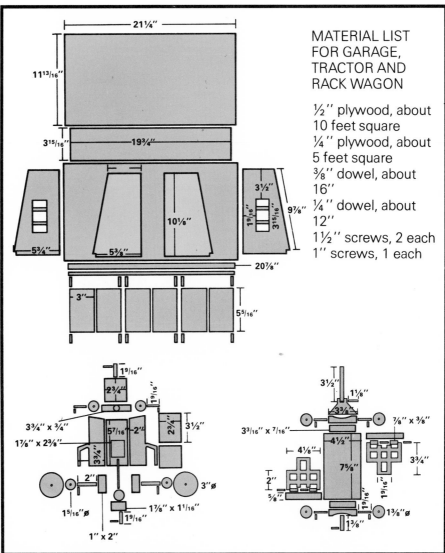

MATERIAL LIST
FOR GARAGE,
TRACTOR AND
RACK WAGON

½'' plywood, about
10 feet square
¼'' plywood, about
5 feet square
⅜'' dowel, about
16''
¼'' dowel, about
12''
1½'' screws, 2 each
1'' screws, 1 each

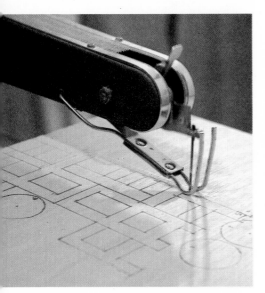

Anyone who has worked on small models before probably recognizes this power tool: a coping saw. With it, all laid-out parts can be cut out quite fast. Of course, a hand coping saw will do the job, too; it just takes longer. The cut-out parts must be glued together (see the tractor in above picture). Masking tape will give the necessary pressure until the glue is dry.

Place the hinge dowels in the prepared holes of garage door and crossbeams, and your crossbeams are ready to be glued onto the side walls: your doors should swing freely now. The roof, when glued on, completes the building.

Tractor and Rack Wagon

Our pictures on the left illustrate how to glue the tractor chassis together. The rear wheels are attached to the chassis with ¼ in. x ⅝ in. dowels. Mount the front axle in the center to the chassis with a wood screw. The axle has to be movable for steering.

The same system will be used for the rack wagon. Secure the wheels the same way. The only differ-

In order to have perfectly round wheels, stick a bolt in the centerhole and lock from other side with a nut. Put the bolt in an electric drill, and sand the wheel with sand paper. Place wheel on axle and secure with small dowels.

ence is the axle diamete which is ¼ in.

The wagon's front an rear racks are cut out plywood pieces. Use a co ing saw (see sketch). The racks are tiltable toward t loading area. The tiltin mechanism is just about t same as the garage doo except that the dowels sti out toward the inside. Inse these dowels in four pr drilled square pieces whi are glued to the loadin area. Tractor and wago have a coupling on the re using a ¼ in. dowel for t steerable hitch with a ho on the front. This allows y to arrange a complete co voy.

▲
Last touchup before varnishing: round all sharp corners to make the toy safe.

What child doesn't sometimes forget toys in the wet grass? Use two or three coats of clear varnish (sand between coats) to protect against moisture.

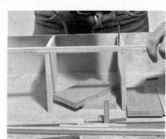

Small dowels enable your garage doors to swing. You will have to drill holes into the roof support in order to insert these dowels.

A humus factory in the garden

This compost box solves the problem of how to dispose of garden waste. You can be rid of the problem of disposal and at the same time gain useful fertilizer for your soil.

The single layers are simply stacked onto each other.

The tips of the corner posts are easily made with a bandsaw. These posts will anchor the box to the ground.

Our compost box of stackable elements uses pine or spruce boards. You may use 1 x 4 or 2 x 4 stock. The dimensions of the compost box shown here are 3 ft. 3 in. x 3 ft. 3 in. If you do not need this much space, you can scale it down. (If you use measurements of 30 in. x 30 in., you will have approximately a third less space.)

Corner-posts are cut from 2 x 2 or 2 x 3 stock to 5 in. lengths; the posts are used to strengthen corners of each stackable unit. For eight layers, you will need 16 boards that are 2 in. longer than the length to be used in the box dimensions, and 16 boards that are 4 in. longer than the side of the box. The first four boards are nailed to the 8½ in. pieces; the longer corner-post length enables the base to be set into the ground. You will then nail the shorter boards to the corner posts, covering

69

about half of each corner support with the boards. The protruding support on the bottom will be about 2½ in. This will leave a 1 in. space between the stacks; the corner post thus also acts as a spacer. The 1 in. spacing is necessary because the decomposition process requires the circulation of air.

The corners are connected with two wood

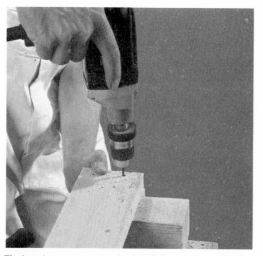
The boards are screwed on flush with the corners, and holes for these must be predrilled. The corner posts are additionally nailed in from the outside.

First, the short boards are nailed onto the corner posts, th eliminating a lot of marking and preventing difficulties when fitting pieces together.

The completed compost box consists of eight layers.

How to obtain good compost

Ripe compost is almost pure humus. There is nothing better to further growth of plant life in the garden. To make compost, alternate layers of garden and kitchen waste (mold) and a mixture of one part peat and one part soil. Before mixing, peat should be thoroughly dampened. (A standard bale will soak up about thirty buckets of water). Lime nitrogen is strewn across each layer to aid in decomposition and to kill weed seeds; it is also a very important nutrient. Be sure to work twigs from trees and hedge clippings into the green mixture. These should be chopped before they are added.

If a compost-starting culture (available at green houses) is added in the fall, the compost will be ready in time for spring planting. The upper layer should always be a mixture of peat and soil. The compost should be turned several times, according to instructions given by the manufacturer of the compost starter.

screws for each board. Predrill the cross-bars and the cross-cut lumber. The screws will prevent a break in the wood. Be sure to use rust-resistant, galvanized screws.

Once the boards have been secured they should be reinforced by putting nails through the corner posts; this makes the entire box more stable. Several coats of wood preservative are necessary, since bacteria that break down leaves and other waste also attack untreated wood.

Prior to use, give the wood two to three coats of wood preservative and sealer, or use redwood or treated wood.

MATERIALS

Treated or redwood lumber preferred.
1 x 4 or 2 x 4:
  16 pcs. 39" long
  16 pcs. 37½" long (if 1 x 4)
            or 36" long (if 2 x 4)
2 x 2:
  28 pcs. 5" long
   4 pcs. 8½" long
64 wood screws (3" for 2 x 4)
                (2" for 1 x 4)
Galvanized nails (16d for 2 x 4)
               (8d for 1 x 4)
Wood preservative (if required)
  2 quarts

Lawn Bowling

Outdoor bowling with a home-crafted set can be an enjoyable sport for the entire family. The stand with the pendulum can be disassembled and taken to most anywhere. Just one rainy weekend or a few evenings will be enough time to make the set, which is so sturdy that it will last for years.

For the bowling pins you will need 126 in. of 3 x 3 lumber; each pin is 14 in. tall. This game has only nine pins, as opposed to the more common ten-pin version. Select well-seasoned lumber without cracks and few knots. Otherwise the pins may split lengthwise in use.

First mark the cuts as seen in the drawing at right. You can cut the grooves with a sash saw if you have no table saw. The pins are chamfered with plane and sandpaper at the edges, more towards the bottom, so that the base of the pin is nearly round. Then they are sanded first with coarse (80) then with fine (150) sandpaper. Then wet and resand with sharp fine paper.

Now you can stain and finish. The king pin is painted a contrasting color so it will stand out.

The game board consists of ⅝-in. particle board. The dots that mark the places for the pins are inlaid slices of dowel. The edge of the game board is framed with half-round molding. The parts for the stand are glued together and also held with screws or dowels to secure the supports. "Nails" of ⅜ in. dowel anchor the stand in the ground; the heads are made of slices cut from ¾ in. round lumber. The angle of the pendulum support is lap joined and fastened with dowels. A row of boreholes together with carriage screws makes the height adjustable. The furniture-foot that serves as pendulum comes from an old armchair. Such turned parts can also be purchased ready-made.

Bowling Without a Bowling Alley

Game board, stand and pendulum alter the well-known game so that it can be played outdoors and on uneven ground.

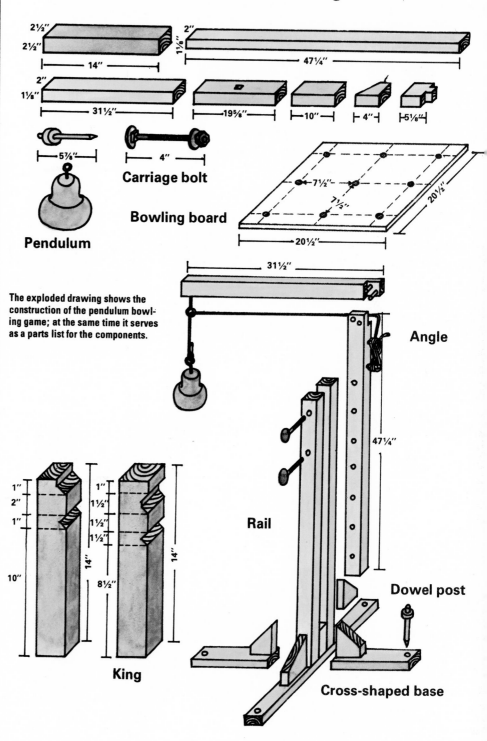

The exploded drawing shows the construction of the pendulum bowling game; at the same time it serves as a parts list for the components.

Here are the materials you will need to build the outdoor bowling set: lumber is used for the pins, dressed roof timber for the pendulum support, ⅝" dowel for the joints and for marking the places for the pins, ¾" round lumber for the heads of the dowels, plus carriage bolts, dyes, the furniture foot and the particleboard.

The detailed photo shows the joint of the vertical supports with cross-shaped base. The center section is set in with a square tenon.

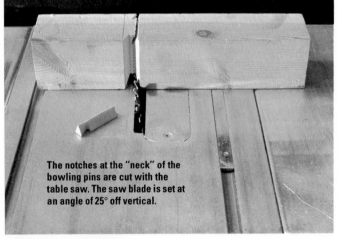

The notches at the "neck" of the bowling pins are cut with the table saw. The saw blade is set at an angle of 25° off vertical.

A finished bowling pin looks like this; here a "pawn." The "king" is emphasized by a second groove and a different color.

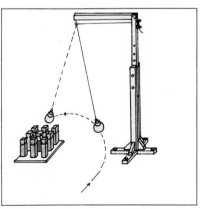

Direction in which the pendulum swings. The game rules: The pendulum may hit the pins only when swinging back. By lengthening the stand and the cord, you can alter the arc and the time of the pendulum swing.

73

This garden furniture of sturdy lumber withstands the strength test.

Bonanza table for your garden

You can make this table using old-fashioned carpentry methods. The material can be redwood, treated Douglas Fir or pine. Use waterproof glue. Treatment should be of the salt method, or "Wolmanized" or "Osmose." Other treatments such as creosote or penta may be hard on your clothes.

You may, if you wish, have the lumber planed and cut at the lumberyard according to our materials list; some lumberyards will provide this service. Choose lumber with an even grain, otherwise it may warp if it is stored in a heated room prior to use. Wood with a spiral grain will twist.

We used 4 x 4 stock square lumber for the base, and 2 x 4 lumber for the tops. The dressed size will be approximately 3½ in. x 3½ in. and 1½ in. x 3½ in. respectively.

The crossed-leg assemblies for table and benches are lap joined in the center.

The crossing angle in both instances is 90 degrees. This results in 45-degree angles at the bottom and at the cross-member joints.

Measure the exact cross-section of the dressed lumber and mark the notches for the lap joint accordingly. The depth must be exactly half the thickness of the wood. Make several parallel cuts, with the circular saw set at this depth. The remaining wood can now easily be chiseled away, and you will not have to worry that the chip will break away deeper than intended. This is only a hazard when the grain does not run parallel to

The heavy ranch style is attractive in any garden.

1. First mark the notches for the lap joints of the leg assemblies. Place both pieces of lumber side by side and mark with the aid of a back square. Precision is important for a good fit.

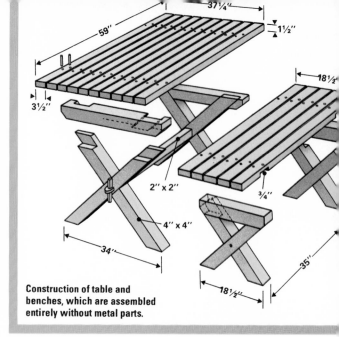

Construction of table and benches, which are assembled entirely without metal parts.

2. The cutting depth of the circular saw is adjusted to exactly half the thickness of the wood. Several parallel cuts are made at close intervals to facilitate subsequent chiseling.

the cut edges of the wood.

On the exploded drawing, as well as in photo 10, you can see the leg assembly of the benches. The corresponding details of the table leg assembly are seen in photo 11. These table parts are designed to be stable even when assembled without glue, as long as they are fitted accurately. The cross-members of the bench supports are fastened with ¼-in. dowels. Waterprooof glue is used for all glued joints—the garden furniture will therefore remain sturdy even after a rain. The boards for seats and tabletop are designed to

be spaced about ¼ in. apart, which allows water to run off. All sharp edges are chamfered with plane or sandpaper prior to assembling the furniture. Where the lumber is cut or notched, it is best to paint on some of the same type of preservative used on the wood. You should, however, avoid areas that will take glue; use a mask for these areas.

A 2 x 2 for the center rail connects the leg assemblies of the table. It is joined with a tenon and a peg. Saw ⅜ in. off the thickness of the wood on both sides, for a length of 6

3. The wood between the saw cuts is removed with a sharp chisel. The depth of the cuts serves as a guide. The wood between the cuts has to be completely removed. A final sanding will aid fit.

4. A tight fit makes for a sturdy joint. Clamps aid in joining the parts; insert wood scraps between clamp and wood to prevent marring of the furniture surface.

MATERIALS

Square lumber, pine or spruce

4 x 4: 4 each of 46''
(table legs); 8 each of 24''
(bench legs); 2 each of 40''
(table, cross-members);
4 each of 20'' (bench, cross-members); 2 x 4: 20 each of
60'' (table, bench tops); 2 x 2:
1 of 44'' (table, center rail);
26½' of ¼'' dowel;
waterproof glue; wood
preservative.

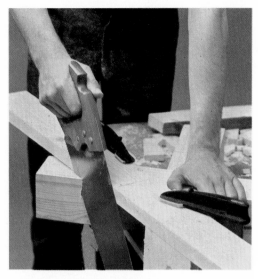

5. The mitered ends on the legs are best cut with a good hand saw. A stop-board clamped in place serves as a guide.

6. Cut so the marking line still shows, to ensure a tight fit. Mark the notches on the cross-members.

The lined parts of the wood have to be sawed and chiseled off. The required w cuts are best made with a well maintained finetoothed handsaw.

8. If the parts do not fit really tight, the joint is also secured with a dowel. Drill a ¼'' hole, apply glue and pound in dowel.

The oblique cuts across the shanks of the leg assembly can be made with a cular saw. The tightly clamped piece of wood serves as guide-stop. Saw depth uals half the thickness of the wood.

10. The crossed-leg assembly and the cross-member are ready to be assembled. The areas which will be glued together have to butt tightly; a dowel gives additional hold.

77

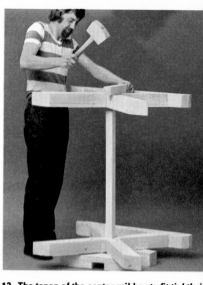

11. These are the components for the table base: in front, the center rail with pegs and then the components for a leg assembly; in rear, the finished leg assembly.

12. Draw the cross-section of the rail tenon at the intersecting point of the legs, drill several holes and chisel out the remainder.

13. The tenon of the center rail has to fit tightly in the hole. This has to be fitted by trial; the tenon m need to be trimmed.

in. at each end. This leaves a tenon 1 in. thick and 1½ in. wide. The width of the tenon must be cut parallel to the grain; if the lines run vertical, the tenon will break off when the hole for the peg is cut out.

Where the legs intersect, make a hole with drill and chisel out the tenon.

The boards for the ta-

bletop are doweled onto the leg assemblies from above. For the benches, the boards also must be notched to half the depth of the material; this provides additional lateral support for the leg assemblies.

The finished furniture should be painted with another two or three coats of preservative.

14. After the table base has been assembled, secure the tenon with a peg. Th required hole in the tenon has been cut with a sharp chisel prior to assemb Some fitting work is required here.

15. The boards for the table and seat tops are finished on all sides, prior to being attached with dowels. The areas to be glued must be covered with masking tape.

16. The staggered dowel holes are drilled into the boards for table and bench tops, using a drill template.

17. Small wedges ensure the right spacing. The drill holes into the base, apply glue, and pour dowels in.

78

If your two-leg horse gets too tired and the sun becomes too hot, the wagon doubles as a cozy, shady playhouse.

A covered wagon for a child's world

This covered wagon can be both toy and transportation. The construction is simple and sturdy, and will survive Indian battles as well as shopping trips.

The wagon consists of four construction units: wagon body with railing, rear axle, front axle with steering, and canopy. The body is built first. Rabbet the side boards and the end boards for a box joint and screw the tenons of the end-boards together with the side boards. Now attach the bottom boards, spaced ¼ in. apart. Do not forget the cut-outs (1½ in. x ⅝ in.) in the center boards (7 in. from the front); the square washer for the steering bolt has to fit in here. After you have attached the railing as shown in the drawing, the body of the wagon is finished.

Next, assemble the rear axle. Cut-outs at right and left are 3⅛ in. long and 1 in. deep. The half axles are placed into the U-shaped groove and screwed to-gether with the axle supports. The front axle is also cut out at left and right ac-cordingly. In addition, there is a cut-out at the top for the steering board (3¾ in. wide, 1¼ in. deep). The cut-out at the bottom is 2 in. wide and 1¼ in. deep. Now attach the half-axles again in the U-shaped groove. A vertical hole for the steer-ing bolt, diameter ½ in., is drilled through the center. Glue and screw the steer-ing board in place (see photo). Drill the hole for the steering bolt, 7 in. from the rear edge. Then, 2 in. from the front edge, drill a hole for the bolt that holds the wagon shaft (5/16 diameter). Finish by sawing a recess for the wagon shaft: 4¹³/₃₂ in. deep, 1⅜ in. wide. Glue the wagon shaft, attach pull rod and drill the hole for the steering bolt at the rear. Of

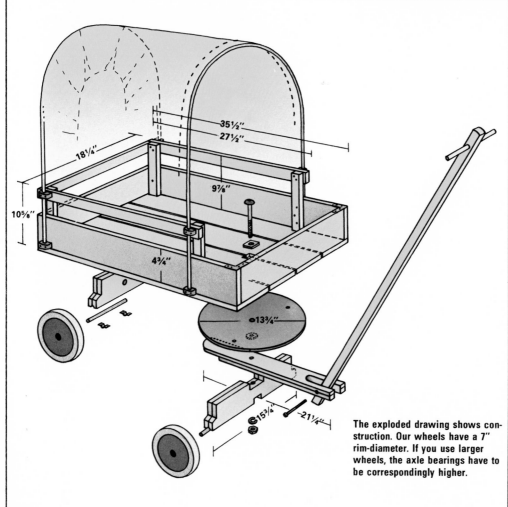

The exploded drawing shows con-struction. Our wheels have a 7" rim-diameter. If you use larger wheels, the axle bearings have to be correspondingly higher.

The finished construction units before they are assembled. The U-shaped cut-out in the rear axle support serves as guide for the half-axle. You can use discarded go-cart wheels or buy new wheels.

Another adventure is always waiting just around the corner.

The finished wagon, without the canopy. Here you can see how the railing supports are screwed together with the guide blocks. The flat angles are additional reinforcement.

◀ This is a bottom view of the wagon; the elastic loops are attached to the protruding screws in the floor boards.

MATERIALS

Pine: 6 pcs.—¾″ x 4¾″ - 35½″, Bottom & Side Rails; 2 pcs.—¾″ x 4¾″ - 18¼″, Front & Back Rails; 2 pcs.—¾″ x 1¾″ - 27½″, Side Railings; 1 pc.—¾″ x 1¾″ - 18¼″, Rear Railing; 4 pcs.—¾″ x 1¾″ - 9⅞″, Railing Supports; 2 pcs.—¾″ x 4¾″ - 15¾″, Rear Axle; 2 pcs.—¾″ x 4″ - 15¾″, Front Axle; 1 pc.—¾″ x 3¾″ - 21¼″, Steering Board; 1 pc. —¾″ x 3¾″ - 16½″, Steering Board; 2 pcs.—¾″ x 1⁵/₁₆″ - 39⅜″, Wagon Shaft; 1 pc.— ¾″ Dia. Dowel - 9″, Wagon Shaft; 1 pc.—13¾″ Dia. - ½″ Plywood, Turntable; 1 Bolt 4¾″ x ½″ with nut; 1 Lock Washer ½″; 1 Bolt 4″ x ⁵/₁₆″ with nut; 1 Washer 1½″ x 1½″; 1 Tarpaulin, 80″ x 40″.

course, the turntable also has to have a ½-in.-diameter hole for the steering bolt. The drawing shows how the wagon is assembled. Rear axle and turntable are attached to the bottom of the body with countersunk screws.

Now attach the guide blocks for the tent poles. Drill blind holes into the lower blocks to the center. Cut a piece of tarpaulin 63 in. long and 39⅜ in. wide and seam all edges 4 in. wide. (The tarpaulin is stretched across the wagon.) Stitch across again, 1³/₁₆ in. from the rear edge. A string is threaded through this "channel" by which the tarp is tightened in rear. At the front edge, and 10 in. from the rear edge, sew channels from the remaining material; each channel is 39⅜ in. long and 2 in. wide and will take the tent poles. Parallel to this, attach on each of the outside edges a grommet (flexible loop) and sew on small triangles of the material as reinforcement. Loops of elastic for attaching the tarp to the bottom of the wagon are pulled through these grommets. The tent poles are 65 in. long and must be flexible. Rods of bamboo or fiberglass, about ⅜ in. in diameter, are most suitable.

Building a country w

Any type of stone can be used to construct a natural stone wall, providing the stones are strong enough.

First calculate the volume of the wall, and order your material accordingly. For a double wall with concrete filling, figure half the volume for stone and allow half for concrete, which also serves as mortar between the stones. Depending on the height of the wall, the foundation ranges from 24 in. to 36 in. deep in the ground; it must go below the frost line and be of poured concrete (the cement ratio of the concrete mix should be: one part cement, two parts sand, three parts gravel). The foundation should be wider at the foot than at the upper end, and should reach to the surface of the ground. The concrete should be damp, but not runny. In loose earth, we recommend that the sides of the foundation be supported with form boards. In solid ground, on the other hand, concrete may be poured immediately. If the wall will be higher than 3 ft., metal reinforcing should be used. The necessary rods or welded matting are put vertically into the wet concrete at the time you pour the footing.

For the core and construction of the wall, a cement mortar mixture of one part cement to four parts sharp sand is used; some slaked lime will make the mortar work more smoothly. Another possibility is to use ready-mix mortar for the stones, and regular concrete for the core.

Before embedding the stones into the mortar, clean them thoroughly so they are free from all grass, clay and dirt. Otherwise the mortar may not adhere. If stones must be chiseled and split, do so in the direction of the veins in the stones; in several types of stones these veins are clearly visible. Make a groove to mark the splitting line, using the cutting edge of a hammer or a chisel. Take a mason's chisel or a mason's hammer and keep cutting back and forth until the groove is ⅛ in. to ¼ in. deep. Stone masons, by the way, call this a "pivot". In fitting the stones together you must do a little sight adjustment until they fit.

Build yourself a natural stone wall; the work will require some effort, but once built it will last for centuries. The uneven and casual structure has its own special appeal and, as long as you adhere to a few rules, nothing can go wrong.

First, cut a groove along the line the stone is to be split, using the cutting side of a mason's hammer.

Then turn the stone over on a solid surface and tap along the opposite side; the end that you want to break off should project beyond the surface.

Sharp tips and edges can be chipped off with light taps of a hammer.

A large selection of stones should be stored close to the work area.

No eyesight is as good as a plumb line. The exact run of the wall must be marked with a chalk line which has been stretched between stakes. On protruding corners, working and placing of stones is very important.

Stones that are covered with grass, clay or dirt must be thoroughly cleaned with water and a brush.

Lightly embed the stones into the moist mortar bed with a few gentle taps of a hammer.

Construct the wall by working on both sides at the same time. Fill the space between with cement mortar.

The top of the wall can be finished off with armored concrete rounds.

83

A simple, attractive planter

This inexpensive, attractive planter can be easily built in just a few hours. It will offer the home gardener many lasting years, because it is made of treated, durable lumber that withstands wind, weather and decay.

The rustic planter is built in two parts; each consists of four 2 x 6 or 2 x 8 members 36 in. long. (Pictures show European lumber of 2 in. x 6⅝ in. actual, so you can take your pick of U.S. sizes (2 x 6 is smaller, 2 x 8 wider than that shown). These pieces are held together by dowels.

This system can also be used to build planters of different shapes and dimensions. For corners other than right angles, the notched end has to be adjusted and the dowel holes relocated.

Where pressure-treated wood is not available, untreated wood can be painted with 3 or 4 coats of wood preservative before assembly (after cutting, notching, drilling).

First cut the notches into the ends of the planks; cut them to half the height and four inches long. Clamp the four sides of one section and drill the dowel holes at the corners. This ensures proper fit.

The top section can then be prepared, making sure the holes line up.

On two of the planks for the bottom section, ledgers for the bottom boards should be nailed flush with the bottom edge. Use 1 in. x 1 in. or 1 in. x 2 in. for the ledger. For the bottom, use

These are the components of the planter before assembly. The dowels are inserted all the way through, from top to bottom.

Here is a view of the plank ends. The hole for the dowel should be ¾" for ¾" hardwood dowels. The 2" x 2" square pieces are used to keep the entire planter off the ground.

Construction is simple. Parts are placed on top of each other and dowels are carefully driven through both sections, using a wood piece as a buffer.

Ledgers of 1″ x 1″ or 1″ x 2″ are nailed on two of the sides to receive the bottom boards.

The top section is placed onto the bottom. Note spacer blocks at the corners. Drive the dowels from the top section into the bottom. ▶

Clamps help when adjusting for proper fit and drilling. Cant strips can be nailed in corners for reinforcement.

Plastic sheets are used as a liner. It is best to have a double layer at the upper edge. Perforate the bottom for drainage. ▶

1 x 4 boards spaced about ½ in. apart.

With the bottom finished, the planter can be assembled. The parts of the bottom section are set together to fit. Before putting on the top section, nail 1 in. thick spacing blocks to the bottom section, as shown, with galvanized or aluminum nails.

The top section can now be set on the bottom section. The dowels are driven through the top section to protrude slightly and to help with alignment. Use a piece of wood as a buffer on top of the dowels to prevent damage with the hammer. Finally, nail 2 in. x 2 in. triangular cant strips in the corners with rustproof nails as a reinforcement.

The planter is lined with plastic. Heavy duty plastic trash bags can be used for this purpose. Punch drainage holes in the bottom of the plastic. Two pieces of 2 in. x 2 in. are set underneath the planter when it is set up to keep it off the ground.

This drawing shows an overview of the construction. The dimensions can be changed to suit. ▶

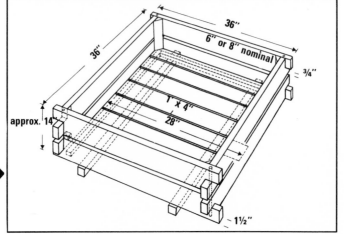

Be creative with Paving Stones

The prettiest mosaics can be created stone by stone in a bed of sand.

Grass around trees can dry out and recede. Paving stones provide a decorative solution.

In your yard or lawn paving with stone can offer a delightful contrast to concrete and asphalt.

Paving stones can be found in deep blue, anthracite, light grey, or even in reddish tones. With this variety, a little gaiety can be brought into your garden. For walkways, patios, or decorative borders, patterns can be created with paving stones. Paving is heavy work, so don't be overly ambitious. Take your time working; if you go too fast, muscle stiffness will soon set in.

One ground rule should be observed: The stronger the load the more solid the foundation must be. Another important note: Stones can be affected by

The walkway to your house can become something special.

Your house number can be inscribed with paving stones on an embankment. In this case it is not possible simply put it on a bed of gravel. A brace has to be put in, and the stone must be embedded in cement, as sand or gravel would be washed away during rain, leaving the whole design to cave in.

A unique house number.

Decorative, weather-resistant and sure-footed, here is a walkway to the front door. First dig out the bed to a thickness of the stones, plus 2" for sand pebbles or gravel. Even when digging the bed sloping should be taken into consideration so that rain water will drain off well. Border the bed with granite stones that are approximately 4" x 4" x 4" and use them also for areas between the pattern. Start at the steps and continue ring by ring; the stones for the round pattern should not be larger than 2" x 2" x 2", otherwise the joints will be too large.

Enlarge your patio decoratively.

Create a colorful patio, or put a decorative edge around an existing one, using walkway tiles combined with paving stones. Here, too, a light slope beginning at the edge of the wall must be planned in so that rain water can drain off properly. Tiles and paving stones should be of the same thickness (about 2"). After laying them, they should be straightened with a straightedge or board. The paving stones should be on a level with the lawn, making it easier to mow, and at the same time protecting the mower.

A sturdy attractive driveway.

Here is another combination of paving stones and blocks, used on the driveway leading to the garage. The foundation must be very solid; for the previous projects a bed of pebbles and gravel is sufficient, but for the driveway a concrete base of 4″ to 11″ in thickness with steel matting for reinforcement would be better. Care must be taken with the foundation so that frost cannot break up the drive in the winter time. Air-entrained concrete, easily available, will prevent this problem. For the same reason, and to prevent washout, adequate drainage should be carefully planned. The slope should be such that water from a cloudburst can easily run off. The concrete blocks for the drive should not be thinner than 2″. When finished, concrete blocks and stones should be lightly tamped in. Any concrete you pour yourself should be cured (kept wet) for 5 days.

Using your imagination with paving stones.

Left: Circular paving with self-formed homemade cement stones. Work from the center outwards. Right: Granite stones combined with brick or clinker.

frost; some that are impervious to frost are available, so watch for this when purchasing them. What good is the best foundation and well-planned drainage, if the stones themselves break up.

On all surfaces, plans must be made for sloping so that rain water drains off fast and well. Otherwise, the sand between the stones will be washed away and tilted stones can easily cause accidents.

The pictures on these pages are offered as a guide; you will undoubtedly have design plans of your own.

atio combinations of granite tones, brick, clinker and tiles.

A pretty diagonal pattern of the same materials.

Exact workmanship is necessary. To lay the patio in the round pattern, small support strips were put in.

Paving with Boulders

Large paving stone, granite

Small paving stone, granite

Basalt mosaic

Granite mosaic

Porphyry mosaic

White quartzite mosaic

Putting in boulder paving is strenuous, but is not technically difficult. The work presents no obstacles or problems that an experienced do-it-yourselfer cannot overcome. We will show you how it is done, and what to watch out for while paving.

Before the stones can be put down the area must be measured and stake out with string. Grass and humus layers must be neatly cut and removed. If the humus layer is thin, sand can be put on top to make a bed for the stones. If it is deep, then pea pebbles or gravel must be added and tamped down and, in order for rainwater to drain off well, the paving must have slight slope. A layer ⅝ in. to 3⁴/₅ in. per 3¼ ft. should be sufficient. In free lying walkways, the sloping should be from the center to the edge. If the walk abuts a wall or building, the incline should start on the adjoining side. To give the paving more solidity, a mixture of cement and sand (1 part cement to parts of sand) can be used; this mixture must be kept moist for 5 days covering the surface with wet burlap an easy curing method.

1. First the humus layer must be removed. If the ground contains water, drainage must be planned for in the foundation.

2. Tree roots in the building area must be removed entirely. It won't harm the tree if a few of the surface roots are cut off.

3. A 2"-thick layer of sand is added on top of the tamped down gravel. The foundation must be measured in such a way that the finished paving surface is of the same height as the surrounding area.

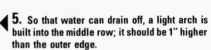

4. The stones are put down adjoining each other in rows. Because of the unevenness of the stones, some slippage will occur.

5. So that water can drain off, a light arch is built into the middle row; it should be 1" higher than the outer edge.

6. Each stone should be tamped into the sand bed with a hammer. Add or take away sand from underneath as needed; sand between the stones must be compressed tightly.

7. When all stones have been laid, toss fine sand over the entire surface area. Distribute the sand into the crevices between the stones by sweeping it in a criss-crossing motion over the surface.

8. Easier yet, this can be done with a water hose, washing the sand into the joints; if necessary, add more sand.

Let your children in on the joys of homeownership. Our fort is solid and will be the pride and joy of any youngster. You will have a reason to be proud, too, because anyone who has built our playhouse has shown the ability to do some serious carpentry work.

The fort in the garden for little adventurers

To give you an idea of how big it is: this playhouse is 100 in. long and 78 in. wide. The inside room will be 81 in. high and the peak of the roof gable is 122 in. high. But don't let the size scare you; if you carefully study our illustrations and enjoy carpentry work, you should have no problems. Our sketch two pages over doesn't give any dimensions; we did that on purpose. This will give you the chance to build the house according to your need (number of children, space in your backyard). You can write your own dimensions on this sketch and order your material accordingly. Or use the materials list given, which indicates quantities that will enable you to build the size shown here.

First cut all the parts, then lay out all notches and overlaps as indicated in photo series. Cut in and chisel; work as precisely as possible. Avoid chiseling

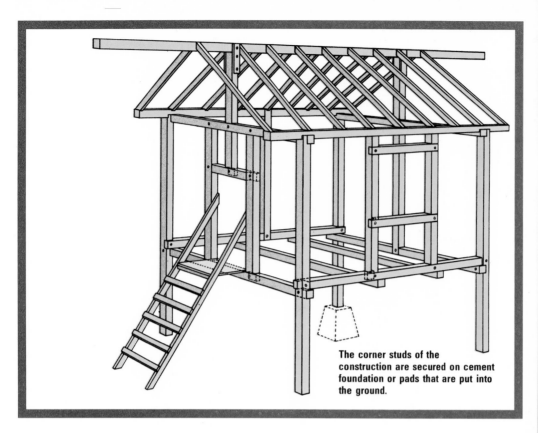

The corner studs of the construction are secured on cement foundation or pads that are put into the ground.

LIST OF MATERIALS

Studs (for stilts and frame): 4 x 4 x 125 ft.
18 Rafters: 2 x 3 (or 2 x 4), 57"
Tongue-and-groove boards: 175 sq. ft.
Plywood panel: 120 sq. ft.
Carriage bolts: 32½" x 5"
Carriage bolts: 18½" x 7"
Carriage bolts: 4½" x 8"

away more than half the thickness of the material. Start assembling the pieces after preparing all the wood this way.

To be sure the fort can endure a storm, rest all four corners of the house on cement posts. Use premix concrete for this purpose. Embed anchor clips so you can attach the stilts. Pay attention so that your four corners are accurately placed, and check that your cornerposts are perfectly level with each other.

To put up the frame you will need helpers. Set and mount the first two corner studs of a narrow side so that they meet at right angles on the cement posts. Screw on the cross-braces, which will later carry the floor boards. Re-

TIP

If overlapping and notching is too time-consuming, there are a series of wood connectors to make the work easier. Shown are Anchor Clips, Framing Clips, Post Base Clips, and Beam Clips; these types of clips are available in lumberyards. (Manufactured by Panel-Clip Co., Farmington, Mich.).

peat that procedure for the other two studs and connect the two narrow sides. Now check again that everything is level; there is still time to correct your cement posts if they need it. Next, mount the upper cross-braces of the narrow sides. Follow by attaching the roof-supporting plates, which have already been notched out (picture 7). Screw from the top with long wood screws onto cross-studs. Build the support construction for window and door frames, using carriage bolts. Now put up the ridge beam (picture 6). Then, notch and nail on the roof rafters, which are 1½ in. x 2⅜ in. studs, to finish the rough construction. After that, take a little time to celebrate.

1. After the concrete is poured in dug-out holes (with anchors), the basic construction consisting of four corner studs and floor construction will be erected.

When it comes to putting up the ridge beam, you will need a strong helper. The beam is put in the prepared supports.

Installing the long floor boards in door opening. Screw a 1 x 4 underneath, so the ladder can be attached later.

3. Drill a ½″ hole in all overlaps and use a 5″ long carriage bolt to attach (our picture shows ridge support).

5. The next three pictures show assembly details. This is an overlap joint of the floor construction. For areas where studs have been notched out less than half of the material thickness, use 7″-long carriage bolts. Use washers with nuts and tighten well.

6. The supports holding the ridge are made of 1″ boards. Three 7″-long carriage bolts are used for a solid connection. The upper end of boards are mitered.

7. The outer support plate is notched and screwed from the top onto the corner studs. Nail on the rafters, which also have to be notched.

8. The upper ends of the ladder are used as handrails. To outlast rough-playing kids, it should be screwed onto the vertical door studs. Nail on the platform. Important: Saw off all bolt ends! Danger of injury!

10. For the final outside paneling, tongue-and-grooved boards are used again. These boards are put together in their tongue-in-grooves, and nailed onto studs on a 40° angle.

9. Doors and window shutters are built of tongue-and-grooved boards. Cut curves with a sabre saw; nail on boards.

Pictures 9-11 illustrate how to build the doors and window shutters as well as how to finish the walls with grooved boards. The roof will be covered with plywood panels that are nailed on. Weatherproof your construction by applying a primer. As the final touch, apply an oil base lacquer. Note the overhanging ridge beam, which is very handy for a climbing rope or a rope ladder.

11. Cover roof with four sheets of plywood. Clamp each sheet first, then nail on.

Hanging Planter

amboo canes, a few yards of chain nd copper or brass rods are the materials needed.

This attractive hanging planter is like an ornament for your window—from lofty heights the flowers float.

This hanging planter can e made quickly, is inexensive, and you can enjoy : for a long time to come ecause the material is so urable. It does not require urther lacquering or other rotective coatings. To build : we used approximately 4-in.-thick bamboo canes vhich were cut into 12-in. engths. The rods (or welding wire) that hold the corers together are ⅛ in. or 1⁄16 in. thick; hard rods of ither copper or brass are est since they do not rust. he planter is fastened bove window with hooks. ecorative hanging greens hat are suitable for planting re green lilies, the entire y family, trailing begonias, nd fuchsias.

On a notched support with a limit stop the bamboo canes can be drilled without difficulty.

The first hole is pushed over the pin. This automatically gives the correct fitting.

The rods that hold all of it together are riveted underneath with a few taps of the hammer.

The canes that form the bottom are fastened with a few wood screws.

At the upper end the rod is bent into a loop into which the chain is fitted.

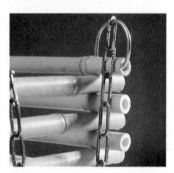

The free end of the rod (or welding wire) is put into a hole which has been drilled into the uppermost cane.

A New lawn game: Giant Dominos

Dominos, the ancient Chinese board game, becomes a fun lawn game. We have painted tiles using a template, and have built two wooden boxes to store and carry the giant game tiles.

You can easily make these giant dominos on a weekend, once you have purchased the required materials. Our design really consists of ceramic game tiles. Glazed tiles are best, if you can find them; 4 in. x 2 in. surface size, ⅝ in. to ¾ in. thick. The tiles are smooth on both sides, and should be available at any well-stocked building materials store or tile outlet. Avoid choosing tiles that have flaws in the surface; an irregular surface means that the template (see illustrations at right) could not be placed flush on top and the color might run. A clean surface is also important, although the tiles need not be of uniform color.

A template, provided with seven ¾-in. holes and the dividing strip are sufficient for marking all symbols onto the game tiles. Just cover those holes not needed for the particular tile; use masking tape. A small amount of paint is applied from above with a brush somewhat smaller than the diameter of the holes.

The boxes in which the game tiles are stored and sorted during the game are made of solid wood boards. They are 16 in. long, 4⅞ in. wide and 4½ in. high. Apply glue at the joints and fasten with screws. Square strips, ¼ in. x ¼ in., are attached

A template is made of hardboard and wood strips to ensure uniform dots. Drill holes with a ¾" wood drill.

Each pattern occurs only once. To mark the 20 tiles you begin with 0:0, 0:1, 0:2, etc. and end with 6:6. The holes of the template not used are, in each instance, all covered with masking tape. The paint (acrylic or enamel) is carefully applied with a small brush to prevent the it from running.

Each storage box has room for 14 domino tiles. Square strips ¼" x ¼" are glued and secured with finishing nails. This keeps the tiles from knocking against each other. The bottom is ¼" plywood.

The handle of 5/4" x ½" hardwood can be folded. A ½" dowel set into the side serves as stop.

Mixing the game tiles: spread all tiles on the lawn, mix with eyes blindfolded, and sort into the boxes. Then flip coins to select boxes. ▶

with glue as spacers and keep the tiles from knocking against each other and chipping, or the painted dots from scratching off.

The 13¼-in.-long handles, connected by a 4 in. dowel, are attached so they can be folded down. One wood screw each provides the pivot point, which has to be ½ in. from the center so that under load the handle is pressed against the stop. The space from the top edge of the box to pivot point is 1¼ in. One wooden dowel, on each side, serves as a stop. Because this game is used outdoors, a water-resistant coating on the plywood will have to be used for the bottom, which is fastened with wood screws. All parts of the boxes are painted with wood preservative so they will be weather resistant.

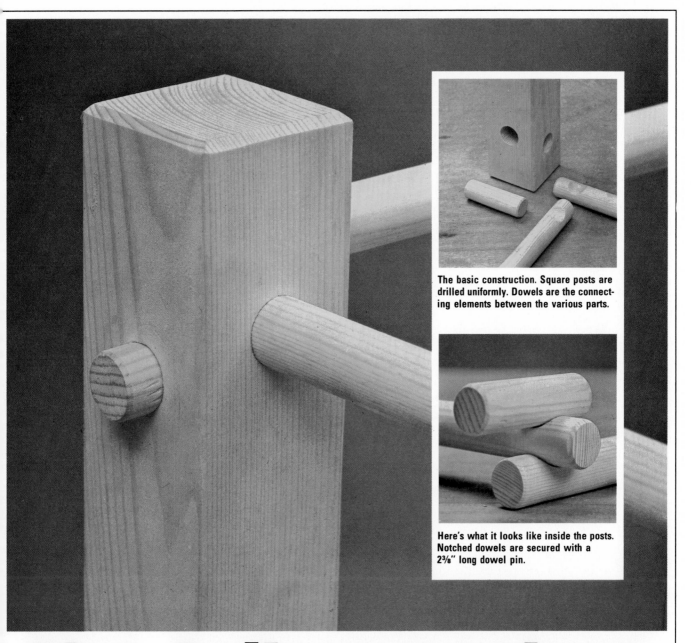

The basic construction. Square posts are drilled uniformly. Dowels are the connecting elements between the various parts.

Here's what it looks like inside the posts. Notched dowels are secured with a 2⅜" long dowel pin.

The *Selbermachen* Dowel System

Furniture building without glue, screws or nails! Yes, it can be done! With a dowel system developed by *SELBERMACHEN,* square parts are connected by dowels and secured by locking dowel pins, much like the corners of a log cabin. Many sturdy, functional pieces of furniture can be made. Illustrated here are three items that show the possibilities of this ingenious system.

Cabinet and chair,
two entirely different
pieces of furniture,
are made from the same
construction system.
With the aid of the
drill template
this and a number of
other furniture pieces
can easily be made by
the homeworker.

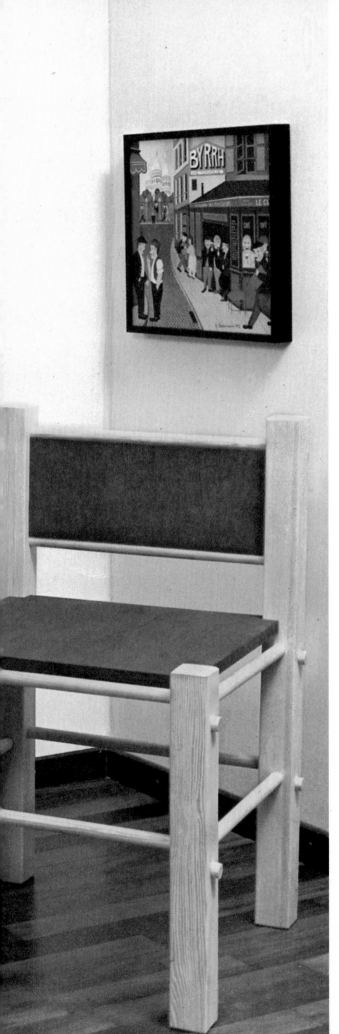

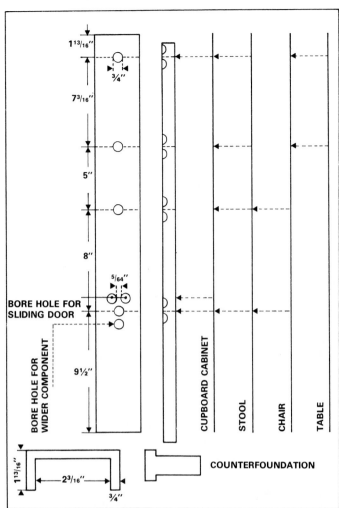

Making this drill-template is essential for our modular construction system. In three examples we show you a number of interesting applications for building various pieces of furniture.

"First drill, then build" is the motto of the *SELBER-MACHEN* dowel system. The standard materials, square posts, dowels, and plywood or veneered particleboard, can be efficiently made into furniture with the aid of a template and drill press. These items of furniture are strong and can easily be disassembled, since they are neither screwed nor glued together.

Use ¾ in. plywood for the drill template. Cut two strips 31½ in. long. One is 2¼ in. wide and the other 3⅝ in. These two plywood strips are drilled with a ¾ in. drill or wood bit as shown in the drawing above. The 2³/₁₆ in. wide strip is sawn into two 1¹/₁₆ in. strips (about ⅛ in. is lost to the saw kerf) after drilling.

The basic materials: square lumber 2³/₁₆" x 2³/₁₆", ¾" dowels, ¾" plywood. Also saw, drill, square and mallet.

Tool for pulling dowels out: two square pieces of lumber 2" x 2" nominal, 6" long, are connected with canvas webbing.

103

Correct handling of drill template

The template (see text for instructions on how to make template) is also used as the length standard. At 37½", it is a frequently used length in the Selbermachen system.

Place template flush onto the square wood and drill 1³¹/₃₂" deep with a ¾" bit in the drill press. Insert locking dowel pin into this hole (see below) and drill remaining holes with the aid of the template. This gives us the precise fit when the elements are assembled. Note: Dowel pins with a head as shown are not required.

A dowel is inserted into the first hole drilled. The square piece is then turned once and the template moved up by ⁹/₁₆". It now rests with the half-round cut-out on the dowel. By staggering the holes the individual dowels are locked into each other.

These are glued to the top of the wide template so that the half-round cutouts, resulting from splitting the ¾ in. holes, point outward. The space between the template sides corresponds to the thickness of the square material. **Caution:** *here is one of the difficulties of translating Metric to English dimensions. In the U.S. you may have to resize the template to the stock or vice-versa.*

The square lumber, since it is not a standard U.S. size, will have to be made for you by a local millwork house. Or you may buy truck stakes or 4 x 4 (3½ in. x 3½ in.) lumber to cut it yourself if you have the equipment. Cut lumber to the proper lengths.

Place the template flush over the square piece and drill the first, outer hole. (All holes are blind holes 1³¹/₃₂ in. deep. Adjust drill press accordingly.) Insert a locking dowel pin into the first hole. It will keep the template from slipping and you may now drill the remaining holes.

Rotate the square piece 90°. Insert a dowel into the first hole on the side. Place the template so the half hole cutout rests on the dowel (see bottom picture). This will offset the template ⁹/₁₆ in. from the end. Drill the holes. If you insert dowels in the holes drilled earlier, before drilling these holes you will also cut out the notch in the dowels.

The next step is to drill the holes for the locking dowel pins. The square piece is rotated again, a dowel inserted into the hole last drilled. The template will now be offset 1⅛ in. Drill the holes for the pin, and the notches in the dowels.

Chair and Stool

The operation of the drill template has been described. This principle applies to all furniture. Once all the square pieces have been correctly predrilled, mount the horizontal dowels (seen from the front on the chair shown) between the square legs. Check that square elements are parallel! Then redrill the holes again with the ¾ in. bit for the side dowels. This puts a groove into the dowel which has already been inserted, into which the side dowel is inserted to check. The same process is re-

Material required for one stool: square lumber 2³/₁₆" x 2³/₁₆"— 4 pieces 19¾" long; ¾" dowels: 8 pieces 19⅝" and 8 pieces 2⅜"; ¾" plywood: 1 piece 20¹/₁₆" x 20¹/₁₆"; Note: You may wish to use veneer edge tape for finishing edges.

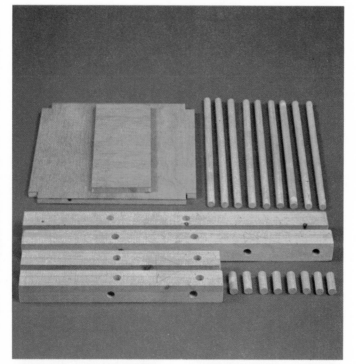

Material required for one chair:
Square lumber 2³/₁₆" x 2³/₁₆": 2 each
31½" long and 2 each 19⅝". Dowels,
¾": 9 each 19⅝" and 8 pieces 2³/₈".
Plywood, ¾": 1 each 18⅝" x 18⅝"
and 1 each 15¹¹/₁₆" x 6½".

eated for the dowels on
e side of the chair. The
cking dowel pin is in-
erted into the groove of
e side dowels. The seats
plywood are first notched
the corners to fit snugly.
ey rest on the top cross-
owels.

The back of the chair, also
ade of plywood, is routed
top and bottom edge to a
alf-round channel (see
oto next page, top right)
d fits tightly between the
owels.

**The two uprights of the chair-back
are now assembled. Rebore and insert locking dowel pin.**

**Assemble front and rear of chair. Re-
bore in the predrilled holes for the
locking dowel pins.**

**The locking dowel pins are inserted
and driven in to a stop with a slight
tap of the mallet.**

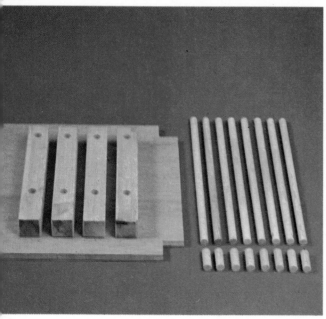

Materials required for this table:
2³/₁₆" x 2³/₁₆"—4 pieces 31½" long;
¾" dowels—8 pieces 35⁷/₁₆" long
and 8 pieces 2⅜"; ¾" plywood—1
piece 35⁷/₁₆" x 35⁷/₁₆" and 4 pieces
31½" x 4¾". The plywood for the
table skirt must be routed half round.

Table and Cabinet

These two pieces of furniture are built on the same principle. Both models require cutting a half-round cove for the vertical facings of the table and the sliding doors. For this purpose the drill press can be used with a half-round router attachment or, use a regular router. You can easily see the detailed layout of the dow-

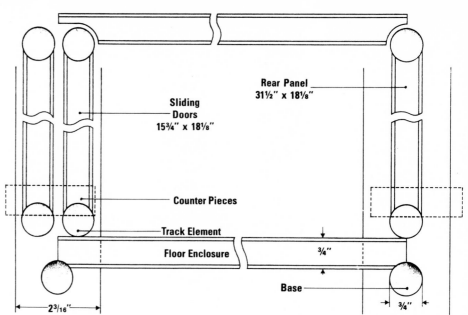

Rear Panel
31½" x 18⅛"

Sliding
Doors
15¾" x 18⅛"

Counter Pieces

Track Element

Floor Enclosure

¾"

Base

2³/₁₆"

¾"

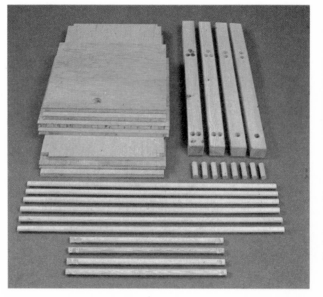

els for the sliding doors of the cabinet in the cross-section drawing through the narrow side of the cabinet.

The cabinet doors slide on dowels. Materials required: square lumber 2³/₁₆" x 2³/₁₆"—4 pieces of 31½"; ¾" dowels, 8 pieces 35⁷/₁₆"; 4 pieces, 19¹¹/₁₆"; 8 pieces, 2⅜", ⁵/₁₆" dowels, 4 pieces ¾" long (the purpose of these is not clear—Ed.); ¾" plywood, 2 pieces 17²⁹/₃₂" x 33¾"; 1 piece 19¼" x 31½"; 2 pieces, 15¾" x 19¼"; and 2 pieces 15¾" x 18⅛".

Easier Furniture Building

Home craftspeople have been waiting for this: an updated version of the time-tested box (or finger) joint. In our version the fingers are cut uniformly so they mesh, rather than having one piece offset as in a "standard" box joint. In our new application, the joint looks completely different, and can be made with a handsaw or table saw with no great difficulty. If the boards you use for the joint are not too thick, several can be cut at once.

The joint is suitable for solid lumber or for lumber-core plywood. That is, the splines that join the fingers can be either plywood or solid stock. You can save time if you use a wobble blade or an adjustable dado blade on a table saw. Or, make several passes with a standard blade. For this latter method you'll need board that acts as a spacer fitted against the rip fence; you make the first pass, then remove one of the boards and make another pass.

Continue until all space boards have been removed. The boards are the thickness of the spacing for the fingers, so you have automatically cut the proper width. Make sure the depth of cut is the same as (no more than) the thickness of the adjoining piece of wood; otherwise the fingers will project and have to be sanded flush. Height adjustment of the blade is critical.

➡

107

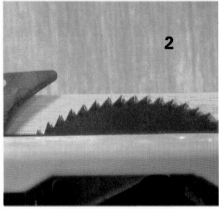

How it's done

1. The glued joint with darker splines can be decorative. If precisely made so the splines fit snugly, and glue is applied carefully, the joint is strong and suitable for the frames of most furniture.
2. Adjust the height of the blade to be the thickness of the stock being used. The advantage of a dado or wobble blade is that every notch and finger will be identical.
3. If the stock being used is not too

thick you can clamp several together and cut the notches in one pass. A good idea is to have a block of wood fastened to the face of the miter gauge that is the exact size of the notch. After you make the first notch against the rip fence, you fit the notch over the block, which is spaced away from the blade the width of a finger, then make another pass over the blade. Repeat.
4. To assure that the splines are glued in straight and meet flush, clamp the assembly between two boards. Never tap directly on the splines, use a block of wood between hammer and wood.

Of Solid Wood

1. Splines of the same wood as that being joined are used here, and are not as prominent as the previous join where a contrasting dark wood was used. The matching wood does show up well for rustic furniture, such as chests and benches. Softwood spline should be much thicker than hardwood or plywood to provide strength.
2. The splines must not be longer than the wood is thick, which eliminates the need for planing and sanding projecting ends. After the boards are glued and joined, lightly sand the end grain of the splines.

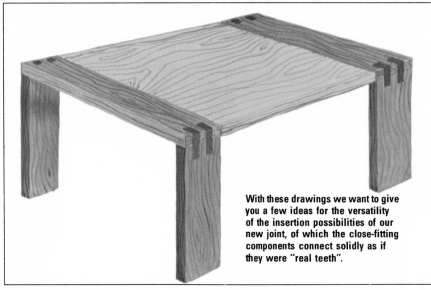

With these drawings we want to give you a few ideas for the versatility of the insertion possibilities of our new joint, of which the close-fitting components connect solidly as if they were "real teeth".

108

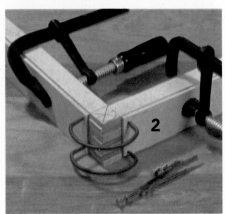

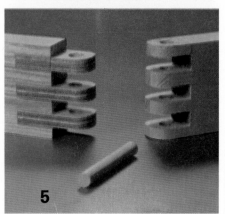

Lumber-Core Plywood

. Plywood can also be joined with he splines. The joint will be strong nough if you space the splines about in. apart. This assembly method is xcellent for shelves and cabinets. It is nportant to apply glue generously to nd grain, as it soaks up the glue. The est bet is to apply a coating of glue, let et a few minutes, apply another coat ist before assembly.

. The splines can be cut from lywood or solid stock of different nicknesses. Solid stock as thin as hown is not readily available, so you'll ave to cut or plane it to suit.

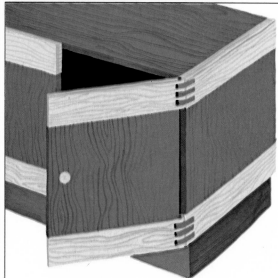

As a Hinge

1. The splines and modified finger joint can be used to create a hinge. Only one side of the splines are glued to one of the pieces. At the other end, splines are left free to pivot.

2. After the splines are glued into one piece, the two pieces are clamped together; the exact center of the corner is marked and a hole is drilled to accept a hardwood dowel. Bore holes in scrap wood to find a bit that will be a snug fit for a ¼ - or 5/16-in. dowel.

3. Double check that both pieces are in precise alignment, then use the correct size bit and drill through the assembly.

4. Clamp parts together at an exact right angle after you have inserted the dowel, then round the corners of the meeting splines and fingers. Pivot the angle in the opposite direction to permit you to reach the unfiled and unshaped section. Do final sanding.

5. This is the finished hinge. The hinge pin may bind at first, but will loosen when worked a few times. A good idea is to rub some paraffin on the dowel before insertion.

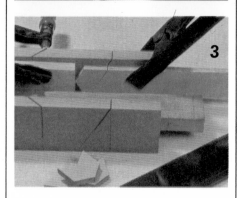

Not at Right Angles

1. Parts that meet at other than a right angle can be joined with the modified finger joint. Hexagons and octagons are assembled in this way.
2. When cutting the notches, be sure that angled ends of the pieces rest solidly on the saw table so the notches are cut the full depth, and correct angle.
3. The arrow-shaped splines are cut from plywood with the aid of a miter box. Cut the arrow shapes a bit oversize, then plane and sand them flush with the surfaces of joined members.

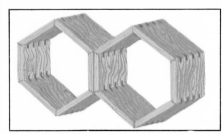

Very Decorative

1. Ordinary laminated plywood makes splines that are extremely attractive, with the several plies showing in strong contrast to the solid lumber. When cutting the plywood splines, use a plywood or planer blade to make sure the plywood does not splinter or chip. Space the splines closely for an especially nice effect—which is ideal on drawers and small chests.
2. Be sure to cut the notches precisely to accept the thickness of the plywood being used. Gaps at the splines weaken the joint, but can be filled with wood filler before finishing.

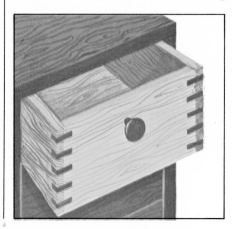

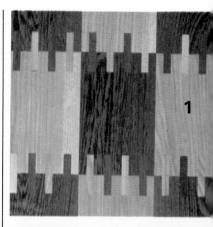

Two Types of Wood

1. For a strikingly attractive table chest top, join squares or rectangles wood of contrasting colors. T splines are cut from the two woo and alternated for the joints to asse ble the pieces.
2. For the project shown, a number pieces were clamped and glued gether with splines. To ensure that t resulting long strips end up flat a straight, be sure that the pieces clamped to a flat surface until the g has set. The strips were then edg glued to create a wide piece of sto

Creating the Jig
for a Finger Lap Joint

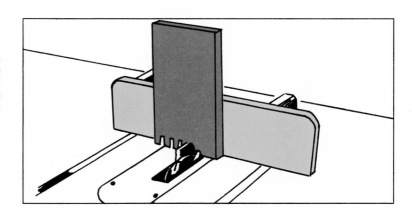

The independent jig is a miter-gauge substitute with twin bars to ride both table slots. Back up the "head" with braces nailed to both the jig and the bars.

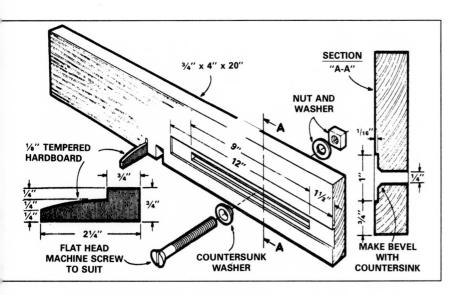

SECTION "A-A"

¾" x 4" x 20"

NUT AND WASHER

⅛" TEMPERED HARDBOARD

¾"

¼"
¼"
¼"

¾"

2¼"

9"

12"

7½"

1/16"

1"

¼"

¾"

FLAT HEAD MACHINE SCREW TO SUIT

COUNTERSUNK WASHER

MAKE BEVEL WITH COUNTERSINK

Adjustable jig provides greater flexibility with finger-lap jointing. Sketch shows details for making this jig.

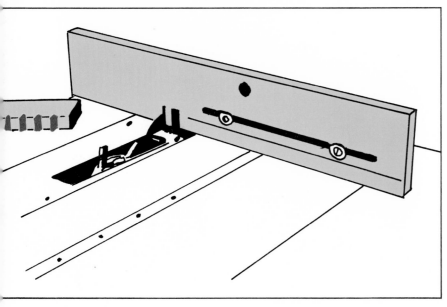

The jig is essentially a piece of 1" stock with cutouts as shown and a piece of ⅛" tempered hardboard as a stop.

Finger
Lap
Joint

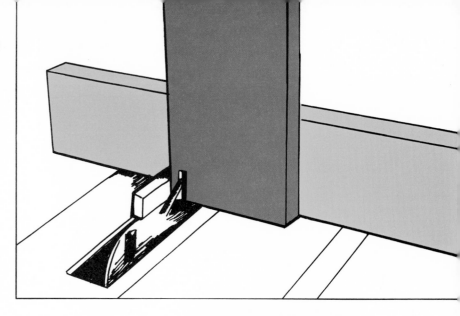

First cut in making the finger lap joint is made by butting one piece against the guide block as you make the first pass.

Place the first cut over the guide block and butt the second piece against it. Advance everything to make the second cut.

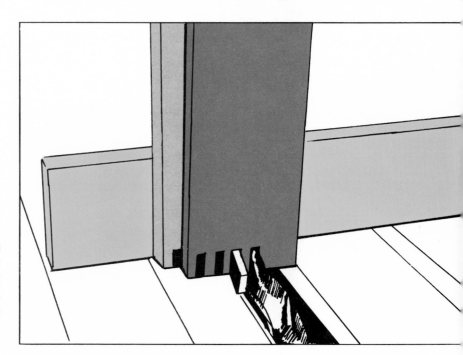

Cuts made are placed over the guide block to position the work for cuts that follow. Throughout the job, be sure that pieces are held firmly together and that passes are made slowly.